CAMPAIGN 263

HONG KONG 1941–45

First strike in the Pacific War

BENJAMIN LAI

ILLUSTRATED BY GIUSEPPE RAVA

Series editor Marcus Cowper

First published in Great Britain in 2014 by Osprey Publishing,
PO Box 883, Oxford, OX1 9PL, UK
PO Box 3985, New York, NY 10185-3985, USA
Email: info@ospreypublishing.com

Osprey Publishing, part of Bloomsbury Publishing Plc.

A CIP catalogue record for this book is available from the British Library.

ISBN: 978 1 78200 268 0
eBook ISBN: 978 1 78200 269 7
ePub ISBN: 978 1 78200 270 3

Editorial by Ilios Publishing Ltd, Oxford, UK (www.iliospublishing.com)
Index by Sandra Shotter
Typeset in Myriad Pro and Sabon
Maps by Bounford.com
3D bird's-eye view by The Black Spot
Battlescene illustrations by Giuseppe Rava
Originated by PDQ Media, Bungay, UK
Printed in China through World Print Ltd.

15 16 17 18 19   11 10 9 8 7 6 5 4 3 2

DEDICATION

To my daughter, Faith Lai.

ACKNOWLEDGEMENTS

I would like to thank Christopher Lai and B. T. Lee for assistance in picture
research, without which this book would not be as interesting as it is. For
help with Japanese translation, I would like to extend my thanks to the
Chen Fei. Finally, I need to thank George Jiao for preparation of the
Japanese War Map.

ARTIST'S NOTE

Readers may care to note that the original paintings from which the colour
plates in this book were prepared are available for private sale. The
Publishers retain all reproduction copyright whatsoever. All enquiries
should be addressed to:

Giuseppe Rava, via Borgotto 17, 48018 Faenza (RA), Italy
www.g-rava.it
info@g-rava.it

The Publishers regret that they can enter into no correspondence upon
this matter.

THE WOODLAND TRUST

Osprey Publishing are supporting the Woodland Trust, the UK's leading
woodland conservation charity, by funding the dedication of trees.

ABBREVIATIONS

ARP	Air Raid Precaution, Air Raid Warden
BAAG	British Army Aid Group
CBE	Commander of the British Empire, British Civil/Military Decoration
CCP	Chinese Communist Party
CO	Commanding Officer – Officer in charge of a Battalion of men
Coy	Company
DCM	Distinguish Conduct Medal, British Military Decoration
DSO	Distinguish Service Order, British Military Decoration
ED	Efficiency Decoration, British Military Decoration
ERC	East River Guerrilla Column
FOO	Forward Observation Officer
GC	George Cross, British Civil/Military Decoration
GOC	General Officer Commanding
HKRNVR	Hong Kong Royal Naval Volunteer Reserve
HKSRA	Hong Kong and Singapore Royal Artillery
HKVDC	Hong Kong Volunteer Defence Corps
IJA	Imperial Japanese Army
IJN	Imperial Japanese Navy
KBE	Knight Commander of the British Empire – British Civil/Military Decoration
MC	Military Cross, British Military Decoration
MP	Military Police
MT	Motor Transport
MTB	Motor Torpedo Boat
NCO	Non-Commissioned Officer
OBE	Order of the British Empire, British Civil/Military Decoration
OC	Officer Commanding – Officer in charge of a Company of men
OP	Observation Post
POW	Prisoner of War
QF	Quick firing
RM	Royal Marines
RMA	Royal Military Academy
RN	Royal Navy
RNVR	Royal Navy Volunteer Reserve
SOE	Special Operation Executive
VC	Victoria Cross, British Military Decoration

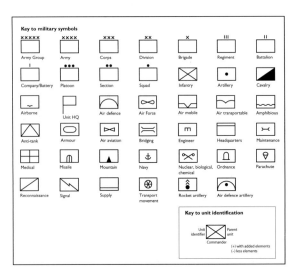

CONTENTS

Japanese plans for Pacific area operations, 1941

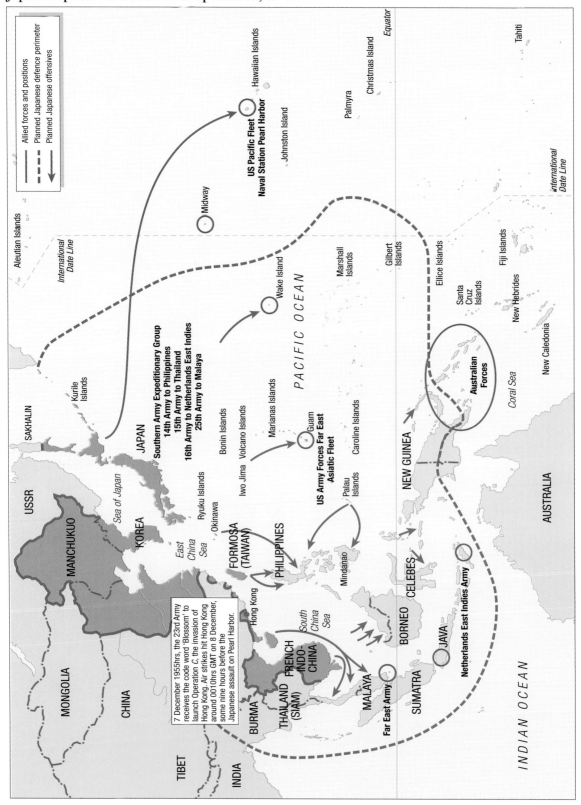

INTRODUCTION

Hong Kong, located at the mouth of the Pearl River in Southern China, came under British administration in 1841 by virtue of the Treaty of Nanjing. The colony expanded from Hong Kong Island to include the Kowloon Peninsula directly to the north and later a strip of mountainous land some 930 sq. km to the north of Kowloon, known as the New Territories. The New Territories are separated from China by a narrow river – the Shenzhen River. Between Hong Kong Island and the Kowloon Peninsula is Victoria Harbour. The colony soon grew from a small fishing settlement into an Asian trading port. All was peaceful until December 1941.

On the 8th, as part of the simultaneous attack on the United States, the Imperial Japanese Army (IJA) also attacked the Philippines, Thailand and Malaysia as well as Hong Kong. Overwhelmed by superior numbers, the British defenders capitulated only after 18 days until liberated by the British Royal Navy under Rear-Admiral Harcourt in August 1945.

As a means of stopping the war in China, the United States imposed crippling trade embargoes on Japan. Reliant on importing 100 per cent of its oil, rubber and many essential raw materials, Japan found these trade embargoes, especially the one on fuel, to be devastating. It was forced to decide between withdrawing from China and going to war to obtain necessary resources, many of them from SE Asia. Japan chose the latter option. With Hong Kong and Manila in the hands of the British and the Americans, the West could hold Japan to ransom by cutting off its vital supply route; thus, securing these ports and protecting the movement of vital war supplies was essential to the survival of Japan.

All-out war with China officially began on 7 July 1937, when the IJA attacked Chinese

A grand view of the city of Victoria, now known as Central District Hong Kong. The large, light-coloured building on the right is the HSBC headquarters; to the north, towards the sea, is the cenotaph and to the right is the Hong Kong Club. (IWM)

A rare picture of the Hong Kong Garrison China Command Headquarters. No trace of this now exists as the location has been totally redeveloped. The site is approximately where the British Consulate, J. W. Marriott Hotel, Hong Kong Park are now located. (IWM)

troops in what was known in the West as the Marco Polo Bridge Incident. The Japanese strategy was to move south after securing Beijing (Peking) and Tianjin and make a separate landing in Shanghai, then head westward capturing Nanjing (Nanking), the capital city at the time. The Japanese expected that after they captured Nanjing, China would then sue for peace and the war would be over. But the Chinese simply moved the government to Chongqing (Chungking) in south-west China and continued to resist. After Chinese victories in Changsha and Guangxi Province in the south-west, the war had reached a stalemate. The Chinese strategy was to buy time and build up the means to sustain the war effort. Much of its aid – weapons, funds and overseas Chinese volunteers – arrived by sea, and Hong Kong was the most important port. By 1940, 40 per cent of military aid, vital supplies and funds received by the Chinese came via Hong Kong. One by one the Chinese ports fell to the Japanese but Hong Kong remained out of reach, as it was a British colony. Cutting off China's supply was therefore critical to Japan's war strategy there.

In the autumn of 1938 the IJA occupied Guangzhou (Canton), the largest city in southern China. British troops soon found that they were eyeball to eyeball with IJA troops across the Sino-Hong Kong border, in what is today known as Shenzhen City. In late 1938 war was only a hair's breadth away.

A British police officer in pre-war Hong Kong. At the out break of war there were up to 5,000 police (including special constables and recently drafted 'specials'). Two hundred and twenty-six of them died both in the battle and the subsequent period of captivity from 1941 to 1945. (IWM)

CHRONOLOGY

1937

7 July	The Marco Polo Bridge or Lugouqiao Incident. Using the pretext of a missing soldier, the IJA attacks the Chinese Army and total war on China begins.
25–31 July	Fall of Beijing and Tianjin.
9 October	Fall of Shanghai.

1938

31 January	Fall of Nanjing (the infamous Nanjing Massacre).
21 October	Fall of Guangzhou.

1939

13, 15, 16 February	Japanese planes deliberately attack border posts as well as British military facilities, causing damage and civilian casualties. Flight of Japanese warplanes over Hong Kong is increasingly common.

1940

June	The Imperial Japanese Navy (IJN) intensifies operations around Hong Kong, harassing fishermen and merchant vessels. The Japanese occupy two of the colony's islands as well as a British lighthouse, imposing a virtual blockade around Hong Kong.

1941

27 October	The Canadian force leaves Vancouver aboard SS *Awatea* and HMCS *Prince Robert* for Hong Kong.
6 November	IJA HQ orders the China Southern Expeditionary Army Group to prepare to attack Hong Kong, with the specific order to begin the operation after landings in Malaysia.

16 November	Canadian reinforcements arrive in Hong Kong.
1 December	IJA is notified of the decision to declare war on the United States, the British Empire and the Netherlands.
4 December	Admiral Sir Tom Philips, C-in-C of Britain's Eastern Fleet, flies back to Singapore from Manila after conferring with MacArthur and Admiral Tom Hart, US Navy, for assistance should Japan attack. Philips comes home empty handed.
7 December	Japanese attack on Pearl Harbor, as well as Guam and Wake Island. All garrison troops are at action stations by the evening.
8 December	0445hrs Hong Kong time, intelligence sources report hearing Tokyo give coded instructions to Japanese nationals that war with Great Britain and the USA has begun.
	By 0645hrs local time, the Hong Kong Garrison has been informed that the British Empire and Japan are at war. Japanese attack on Hong Kong begins roughly, nine hours before the attack begins on Pearl Harbor.
9 December	Attack on the Shing Mun Redoubt late evening. Redoubt falls at 0100hrs, 10 December.
10 December	HMS *Prince of Wales* and *Repulse* are sunk.
12 December	Kowloon Peninsula is evacuated.
18 December	The IJA succeeds in landing and securing a foothold on Hong Kong Island.
19 December	The IJA pushes towards Wongneichong Gap by nightfall and reaches the garden of Repulse Bay Hotel; the 2nd MTB flotilla carries out a suicidal raid on IJA landing boats. WO2 Osborne Winnipeg Grenadiers is killed; posthumously awarded the VC.
25 December	Ceasefire is declared at 1515hrs, and surrender document is formally signed at 1800hrs. That same evening one-legged Chinese Navy Rear-Admiral Chan Chak is given command of the remaining Royal Navy boats, together with 60 survivors, and makes a daring escape by sea and on foot to Huizhou (Waichow) China.

1942

January	The CCP-led (Chinese Communist Party) Guangdong People's Anti-Japanese East River Guerrilla Column (ERC) is established. The guerrillas conduct conventional guerrilla warfare on land and sea, killing traitors and collaborators, rescuing VIPs, gathering intelligence and rescuing downed American pilots.

23 July	British Army Aid Group (BAAG), a China-based MI9 military intelligence unit, is founded by ex-POW Lt. Col. Lindsey Ride HKVDC (the Hong Kong Volunteer Defence Corps) with the aim of providing aid to escaped Hong Kong POWs and downed Allied airmen, and gathering intelligence.
1 October	Systematic transportation of POWs to Japan for hard labour. More than 800 die after the SS *Lisbon Maru*, a Japanese transport ship from Hong Kong, is sunk off the coast of eastern China by a US submarine, the USS *Grouper*.

1943–45

	USAF 14th Air Force's B-25 and, B-24 bombers, escorted by P-40, P-51 and P-38 fighters, begin regular bombing of Hong Kong and of Japanese shipping around Hong Kong waters.

1945

15 August	Japan surrenders.
30 August	Rear-Admiral Cecil Harcourt, Royal Navy, commanding the 11th Aircraft Carrier Squadron, enters Hong Kong waters.
16 September	Rear-Admiral Harcourt takes formal surrender of Japanese forces under Vice-Adm. Fujita and Lt. Gen. Tanaka in the Governor's House, Hong Kong.

OPPOSING COMMANDERS

BRITISH COMMANDERS

Sir Mark A. Young GC MC (1886–1974), 21st Governor of Hong Kong, was Eton educated and commissioned into the Rifle Brigade in World War I. He arrived in Hong Kong to take up his post only three months before the Japanese attack, and spent 1941–45 as a POW. Prior to Hong Kong, Young served in Sri Lanka and the West Indies before taking a post as Governor of Tanganyika.

Major-General Christopher M. Maltby CB MC (1891–1980), GOC China during the battle of Hong Kong, was commissioned into the Indian Army in 1911 and saw service in World War I and the Persian Gulf (1913–14), as well as the North-West Frontier (1923–24). Maltby's early work impressed his superiors and he was selected for fast-tracking to senior positions through staff colleges in Quetta and RAF Andover. In 1937 he once again served on the North-West Frontier and by 1939 he commanded the 3rd Jhelum Brigade, later the Calcutta Brigade, as well as the 19th Infantry Brigade based in Deccan. In 1940, posted to China, he was instrumental in closing the North China Command by withdrawing the two infantry battalions from Shanghai. In August 1941 Maltby was promoted to major-general as GOC China. In the three months of his tenure he set about preparing the colony as best he could; it was a question of too little, too late.

Major-General Arthur E. Grasett DSO MC (1888–1971), GOC China until July 1941 and Canadian by birth, graduated from RMA Sandhurst in 1909 with the Sword of Honour before being granted a commission with the British Royal Engineers during World War I, where he was awarded a

Major-General Christopher Michael Maltby, GOC China, on the left in shorts, is seen conferring with newly arrived head of the Canadian Forces Brigadier John Lawson on the right. In December 1941, Maltby was really a substantive colonel. He became an acting major-general only on 28 April 1941. (IWM)

DSO and MC. Whilst attending the tri-service Imperial Defence College in 1934, he carried out a study which concluded that holding Hong Kong was unjustifiable yet, strangely, in the 1940s, he became convinced that it was, albeit with additional troops. Knighted in 1945, he retired as a lieutenant-general in 1947.

Brigadier Cedric Wallis (1896–1996), Commander of the Kowloon Infantry Brigade (KIB), later East Brigade, enlisted in 1914 as a trooper in the Royal Horse Guards, before gaining a commission with the Sherwood Foresters. Wallis served in France with the Lancashire Regiment, losing an eye. In 1917 he joined the Indian Army and served in Iraq, India and Burma and by 1939 was the commander of all internal security troops in Bombay before being appointed, on arriving in Hong Kong in 1940, CO of the 5/7 Rajputs. After the war, he emigrated to Canada, became a businessman and lived in Vancouver until his death in 1996.

Brigadier John K. Lawson (1887–1941) was Commander of the Hong Kong Infantry Brigade (HKIB), later the West Brigade. He was the highest ranking Canadian soldier killed in action in World War II. Born in Yorkshire he later emigrated to Canada and saw service in World War I with the Canadian Expeditionary Force, enlisting as a private before gaining a commission. Lawson was mentioned in dispatches twice and won a Croix de Guerre. During the inter-war years Lawson continued to serve in the Canadian Army, rising to the rank of colonel. In September 1941 Lawson was made a local brigadier and was given the command of the Royal Rifles of Canada and the Winnipeg Grenadiers bound for active service in Hong Kong.

Lieutenant-Colonel John L. R. Sutcliffe, CO of the Winnipeg Grenadiers (1899–1942), served in the British Army from the 1910s to the 1920s in France, Belgium, India, Iraq, Iran, Russia and Turkey, before transferring to the Canadian Army. Sutcliffe died from malnutrition whilst a POW.

Lieutenant-Colonel William J. Home MC ED, CO of the Royal Rifles of Canada (1897–?), born in Nova Scotia, served with the 8th Royal Rifles in 1913 and later joined the RCR as part of the Canadian Expeditionary Force in World War I, during which he won the MC. In 1939 he was removed as OC of RCR as being 'unfit for command' but, in the 1942 Royal Commission, Home's performance was seen as above par and he was described as an 'excellent officer'. Home was promoted to brigade commander after the death of Lawson. Home survived the war and ended his career as a brigadier in the Canadian Army.

Colonel P. Hennessey was originally a native of Cork, serving in the ranks in the British Army before emigrating to Canada just before World War I. He joined the Canadian Army and was noted for his ability and pushed through officer training. After World War II, Hennessey took up a senior position in the National Defence Headquarters.

Sir Mark Aitchison Young (1886–1974), 21st Governor of Hong Kong. Young was initially held in the Peninsula Hotel and subsequently incarcerated in Stanley Prison, before being transferred with other senior captives to camps in Shanghai, Taiwan, Japan, and then liberated from north-east China in 1945. (Hong Kong Library)

Colonel Henry Barron Rose MC was commissioned into the Wiltshire Regiment in 1911. He served on the Western Front as well as in Russia during the Bolshevik Revolution. Rose won an MC whilst a captain in a daring escape from captivity during World War I. He was seconded to command the HKVDC in August 1938 and promoted as local colonel on 14 September 1941. (Hong Kong Library)

Enthusiastic for action, several senior Canadian officers took a drop in rank in order to join the expeditionary force. Second-in-command **Lt. Col. John H. Price OBE MC ED**, son of Sir William Price, one of the richest businessmen in Quebec, joined the Hong Kong expedition after making strenuous efforts to lobby the Minister of National Defence C. G. Power, to select his regiment for a foreign expedition. A gunner by trade, Price volunteered to take a drop in rank to major to rejoin the Royal Rifles of Canada as the battalion second in command. **Lieutenant-Colonel Tom MacCauly DCM ED** was the CO of the Sherbrooke 7/11 Hussars. He too, took a drop in rank to become OC of B Coy, Royal Rifles of Canada. **Lieutenant-Colonel C. A. Young MC ED**, a veteran of World War I, took on the job of OC A Coy, Royal Rifles of Canada, and also took a voluntary reduction in rank.

Lieutenant-Colonel Lindsey T. Ride OBE CBE HKVDC (1898–1977), an Australian, saw service at the Somme and was the Vice-Chancellor of Hong Kong University. Ride commanded the garrison's field ambulance units during the battle and successfully escaped captivity by fleeing to Free China. He founded the British Army Aid Group (BAAG).

Rear-Admiral Chan Chak (Andrew) KBE RocN (1894–1949), a one-legged Chinese admiral, came to Hong Kong in disguise but was in fact working as a senior representative of the Chinese Nationalist Government. He did valuable work in eliminating fifth columnists and spies. His claim to fame was to lead the famous escape to Free China on Christmas Day 1941. For this, Chan was awarded an honorary KBE.

Commander Zeng Sheng (1910–95) founded the ERC in 1938, under the direction and support of the CCP. In 1955 Zeng was awarded the rank of brigadier in the PLA and was appointed as deputy commander of Guangdong military district and later Deputy Provincial Governor and Minister of Transport.

Sergeant Gander, the unofficial mascot of the Royal Rifles of Canada, was a Newfoundland dog, posthumously awarded the Dickin Medal, the 'animals' VC', in 2000 for his deeds in World War II (the first such award in over 50 years). He is seen here en route to Hong Kong. (Author's collection)

JAPANESE COMMANDERS

Lieutenant-General Sakai Takashi (1887–1946), son of a factory worker, was a China campaign veteran who rose to become the commander of the 23rd Army. He was ordered to use the 38th Division, which normally came under the Southern Expeditionary Army Group, to capture Hong Kong. Sakai served as Governor of Hong Kong from 26 December 1941 to 20 February 1942.

Major-General Kuribayashi Tadamichi (1891–1945), best known as the Japanese commander during the battle of Iwo Jima, graduated from the Army Academy in 1914, specializing in cavalry. He was appointed as deputy military attaché to Washington and Canada and also studied at Harvard University. In December 1941, Kuribayashi was the Chief of Staff of the Japanese 23rd Army.

Lieutenant-General Sano Tadayoshi (1889–1945) was commissioned into the artillery; nonetheless he took command of the 38th Division, the principal invasion force in the battle of Hong Kong. The 38th Division was reported to have committed atrocities against civilians in Hong Kong and British prisoners of war.

Major-General Ito Takeo (1889–1965), born in the city of Fukuoka, was formerly the commander of the 228th Infantry Regiment and later the 114th Infantry Regiment, before being assigned to 38th Division. Ito was Sano's subordinate and commander of the 38th's Infantry Group for the invasion

Kuribayashi Tadamichi, better known as the Japanese commander on Iwo Jima in 1945, was then the Chief of Staff of the IJA 23rd Army in the battle for Hong Kong. According to a former subordinate, Kuribayashi regularly visited wounded enlisted men in hospital, which was virtually unheard of for an IJA general. (Author's collection)

Vice-Admiral Niimi Masaichi, commander of the IJN invasion force, is on the right and Lt. Gen. Sano Tadayoshi, his counterpart land forces commander, on the left, seen here stepping ashore on Hong Kong Island, in the vicinity of Causeway Bay after the surrender of the British on 25 December 1941. (Author's collection)

of Hong Kong. Ito's campaign was characterized by extreme ruthlessness and the massacre of prisoners. He was tried and convicted after the war for war crimes by the Australian Court.

Vice-Admiral Niimi Masaichi (1887–1993) was born in Hiroshima; specializing in naval artillery, he was appointed naval attaché to the United Kingdom 1923–25. In 1936 he accompanied Prince Chichibu to England for the coronation of King George VI. In April 1941 he commanded the 2nd China Expeditionary Fleet, and was responsible for the naval component of the invasion of Hong Kong. He nominally shared the position of Head of Japanese Occupation Forces in Hong Kong with Sakai, but his authority was limited to offshore responsibilities. He retired from active service in March 1943.

Colonel Doi Teihichi (1889–1968) was born in Hyogo Prefecture and graduated from the Military Academy in 1914. Until 1941 he was the 4th Division's director of weapons. Doi's 228th Regiment broke the Gin Drinkers Line by capturing the Shing Mun Redoubt.

Colonel Shoji Toshishige (1890–1974) was a native of Sendai and graduated from the 25th class of the Army Academy. In 1912 he graduated from the Army Staff College and took command of the same 230th Regiment that committed the massacre of St John Ambulance staff and wounded soldiers during the battle of Hong Kong. However, he was acquitted of war crimes. The 230th Regiment, like most of the 38th Division, was decimated in the battle of Guadalcanal.

The 229th Regiment, commanded by **Col. Tanaka Ryosaburo**, committed many infamous war crimes during the battle of Hong Kong, in particular the bayoneting of captured soldiers and civilian personnel. Tanaka was convicted of war crimes and was sentenced to 20 years' imprisonment.

OPPOSING FORCES

BRITISH FORCES

On the eve of war, the British garrison consisted of 13,981 all ranks, including nursing staff and St John Ambulance personnel. Of the soldiers 8,919 were British and Canadian and 4,402 were Indian and Chinese. The actual number of regular infantrymen was 5,422 with approximately 6,000 more serving in the artillery, engineers, the navy and HKVDC (Hong Kong Volunteer Defence Corps). The Royal Navy in 1941 was a pale shadow of the once-powerful China Squadron; of the three World War I destroyers that were in Hong Kong on 8 December, two had been sent away to Singapore (while the third was under repair) by 1930. This was partly to save them from what was a futile defence and partly because of a promise (made by senior US Navy officers) of the assistance in Singapore of four US Navy destroyers in return for Britain reinforcing Singapore with its Hong Kong fleet – a promise that was not to be realized.

The fixed defences were primarily designed to counter an attack from the sea: 29 coastal guns of 9.2in., 6in., 4.7in. and 4in. calibres; ten 18- and 2-pdr beach defence guns; 28 field guns consisting of 60-pdr, 6in., 4.5in. and 3.7in. calibres.

The Hong Kong Garrison infantry force comprised four regular army battalions, two British and two Indian, supported by the HKVDC's five infantry companies averaging 100 men apiece. The 1st Middlesex Regiment (which arrived in August 1937) was a machine-gun battalion with 48 Vickers medium machine guns. The regiment, having been overseas since 1931, had grown stale from 'soft' garrison duties, Hong Kong being one of the softest. From September 1939, all of the regiments, including the 5/7 Rajputs (arriving June 1937) and the 2/14 Punjab, suffered the 'milking' of experienced officers and NCOs to some degree.

The British Empire 'standard' coastal artillery of the day was the 9.2in. naval gun. Hong Kong was no exception. This gun has a range of 25.6km and is capable of two to three shots a minute. This example can be seen in the Imperial War Museum, Duxford. (Author's collection)

British Power Boat 60ft MTBs of the Royal Navy on patrol around Hong Kong waters in 1940. These boats were armed with two twin-mounted Lewis guns, one forward- and one aft-facing, depth charges, and, unusually, two rearward-firing torpedoes. (IWM)

The loss of leadership was especially noticeable with the Royal Scots, which had problems with discipline and an unusually high number of courts martial. These regiments, especially the Hong Kong and Singapore Royal Artillery (HKSRA), lost many experienced officers and NCOs that were not immediately replaced. By the time the Japanese attacked, many of the units were filled with half-trained replacement recruits, which certainly influenced combat effectiveness. The Punjabis were a particularly sad case, having been in Hong Kong since November 1940, but not receiving vehicles and mortars until August 1941. Additionally, 40 per cent of their ranks were raw recruits that had arrived only in October 1941. When the war began, many of the RA regiments had to make do with junior officers taking on senior roles, and British officers, not fluent in Urdu, were forced to command Indian troops, seriously hampering combat effectiveness.

Poor equipment was another problem – shells dating from 1918 that exploded on leaving the muzzle and insufficient ammunition hindered operational efficiency (on 8 December all field guns were deployed with only 100 rounds, with 200 rounds in reserve for the entire campaign, and 25 rounds per gun for the large-calibre coastal guns). Lack of cross-training

Major-General Maltby (in shorts) receiving a salute from the Canadian forces as they arrive in Hong Kong. This picture was taken on the corner of the Peninsula Hotel (in the background) at the junction of Nathan Road and Salisbury Avenue, in Tsim Sha Tsui, Kowloon. (IWM)

A rare picture of ARP workers in Hong Kong. Note the uniforms and the black berets, which are probably Army surplus stock. By November 1941, it was reported that ARP had 1,155 members, not including 300 untrained recruits. Many ARP members were drawn from the scouting movement. (IWM)

meant many of the infantry did not understand the artillery 'clock face' target indication method, causing them to miss their target.

European troops, in particular the Royal Scots, were seriously affected by malaria, as the regions around Shing Mun Redoubt were notoriously badly affected. Of the 770 or so men of the Royal Scots it was reported that at least 180 had recurring malaria attacks. The lack of suitable command staff was a serious problem and almost every unit in Hong Kong had to put junior officers in senior positions.

Although the arrival of the Canadians was a welcome boost to the Hong Kong Garrison, there were handicaps that reduced the combat effectiveness of this force. Both units were classified as C-class, deemed as unfit for foreign service. Years of garrison duties and lack of training compounded the

HMS *Robin* in more peaceful times in Wuzhou, China. Commissioned in 1934 and deployed as a boom ship from January 1941, it participated in the evacuation of HKIB, deployed against the Japanese landing on Hong Kong, was disabled by air attack on the 25th and scuttled after the destruction of classified documents. (Author's collection)

problem. To illustrate this deficiency: the Canadians only fired 35 rounds each in rifle practice. The two battalions received 115 men who had less than 16 weeks' training as reinforcements and, of the 75 raw recruits who joined the Winnipeg Grenadiers in June, 62 joined the Royal Rifles of Canada from a training depot where there was not even a single rifle. Twelve per cent of the Canadians were untrained recruits!

Even worse was the lack of equipment. In 1941 a standard Canadian infantry battalion should have had 102 motor vehicles, including 22 Universal Carriers, 37 ¾-ton trucks, 13 1-ton trucks, 31 bicycles and 22 Boys anti-tank rifles. Logistic incompetence meant that when the Canadians arrived in Hong Kong, they had with them only six Bren carriers, two water tankers, 12 ¾-ton trucks and one Boys anti-tank rifle. There were 3in. mortars but no bombs or radios. Such was the level of preparation for war by Canada in 1941, there were only 300 rounds of 3in. mortar bombs in the whole of Canada at the time, and it was not surprising that none could be spared for the Hong Kong expedition.

A second ship, the SS *Don Jose*, was dispatched with the missing vehicles and equipment but it did not make it to Hong Kong before 8 December and was diverted to Manila where it was promptly seized by the Japanese! Despite these shortcomings the force set sail on 27 October with a total of 1,975 men and arrived in Hong Kong on 16 November.

Intelligence estimates vary, giving anything from two to four divisions of Japanese available for the attack on Hong Kong. On the evening of 6 December Chinese reports showed the arrival the previous day of three Japanese divisions at Buji township, located in the suburb of what is today's Shenzhen City, some 8 miles from the frontier. On 1 November 1941 or thereabouts, a Japanese deserter crossed the border and revealed that there was definitely a build-up of troops north of the frontier and the presence of large-calibre artillery, indicating at least divisional strength.

HMS *Thracian* was an S-class destroyer, laid down in 1918 at Hawthorn Leslie in Newcastle upon Tyne, and entered service in 1922. On 25 December 1941, it was grounded and later scuttled but afterwards raised to become IJN Patrol Boat No. 101. On October 1945, it was returned to the Royal Navy but scrapped in 1946. (IWM)

JAPANESE FORCES

The Hong Kong invasion force consisted of three elements; the IJA committed the 38th Infantry Division, while the IJN committed the Second China Fleet and the 1st Air Group represented the IJAF (Imperial Japanese Air Force).

The main strike force consisted of three infantry regiments of the 38th Division, the 228th, 229th and 230th under Col. Doi Teihichi, Col. Tanaka Ryosaburo and Col. Shoji Toshishige respectively. The 38th Division was commanded by Lt. Gen. Sano Tadayoshi with Maj. Gen. Ito Takeo as head of the infantry group, with the remaining supporting arms such as artillery, engineers, armour, transport, hospital etc. controlled by Sano. The 38th Division was a 1940s standard B infantry division, consisting of some 20,000 troops (this could vary from 18,000–21,000 depending on the task in hand) with three infantry regiments, each with three battalions. The Japanese army in the 1940s relied heavily on animal and human transport. Each regiment had approximately 3,800 troops with some 700 horses, with the battalions each consisting of about 1,071 and the companies of 180. A rifle platoon consisted of four sections, three equipped with rifles and light machine guns and the fourth with light mortars and rifles. Japanese infantry battalions of this era had an additional heavy machine-gun company (12 x Type 92 heavy machine guns) on top of the infantry companies, as well as a troop of light artillery, probably Type 92 70mm infantry guns. The divisional field artillery regiment was equipped with 75mm (Type 41) mountain guns, organized into three 688-man battalions. Each battery had two troops, each with two guns.

A Japanese soldier stands guard overlooking the Lo Wu Railway Bridge that spans the Shenzhen River. The Shenzhen River marks the border between Hong Kong and mainland China. Note the desolate scene around the Lo Wu crossing in 1941. (Author's collection)

The mountain artillery was similarly organized, consisting of 36 75mm guns but, on account of the complexity of mountain operations, these units usually had more soldiers (3,400) and animals (1,400). Realizing the need to shell Hong Kong into submission, the IJA boosted the invasion force with additional artillery – 15cm and 24cm howitzers under Maj. Gen. Kitashima Kineo.

News of the Canadians arriving in Hong Kong caused the Japanese to revise their plan. Lieutenant-General Sakai Takashi, commander of the 23rd Army, was forced to inform his superiors that the ten-day timescale was not realistic and requested reinforcements. This caused something of a problem as most formations had already been allocated to other impending operations, but eventually the Imperial HQ sanctioned two infantry regiments, 5th and 6th depot regiments in Japan, to support the invasion of Hong Kong. These units were not intended for front-line service, but instead were expected to take on second-line duties freeing up more experienced men for the Hong Kong force. They were sent to the 23rd and 13th armies in Shanghai with a clear message for them to return the units as soon as possible. This allowed the 19th and 20th mixed brigades of about 6,000 men in five infantry battalions, a field artillery battalion as well as an engineer battalion to be released to support the invasion of Hong Kong. Sakai learned that his request for troops was not viewed favourably by Imperial HQ and he was given the impression that a swift and effective campaign was essential. It was furthermore embarrassing for him to have to return to Imperial HQ for help after the Japanese agents in Hong Kong mistook the Bren carriers for tanks. Only by raiding the 1st Reserve Tank Battalion and the tankette units attached to the infantry depot divisions was Sakai able to scrape together enough tanks. Sakai also tried to obtain more

Japanese Type 92 medium machine-gun team in action at the Gap. The Type 92 was a 7.7mm copy of the Hotchkiss M1914 machine gun. It had a maximum range of 4,500m, but a practical range of 800m. (IWM)

armour by hijacking the 9th Reconnaissance Regiment from the 11th Army but was thwarted by sustained complaints from Gen. Hata Shunroku of the 11th Army to friends in high places. Sakai was given a sharp reprimand that any more requests would not be entertained and that he would be replaced if necessary! Having lost much face, Sakai dropped all requests for additional troops and was now even more determined to succeed.

The naval element was divided into two parts: the bombardment group and the attacking group. Both were commanded by Vice-Admiral Niimi Masaichi, head of the 2nd China Expeditionary Fleet. Niimi's flagship was the light cruiser *Isuzu* with Ura Koichi as captain, who was also the head of the bombardment group. This naval group was made up of ships scraped together from various units of the China Expeditionary Fleet, particularly from Canton (Guangzhou) Special Base Force, 15 Squadron and 11 Torpedo Boat Division from Guangzhou.

A seaplane tender, IJN *Kamikawa Maru*, was on attachment after strenuous representation by Niimi of the 2nd China Fleet, who did not trust the army to provide air cover and wanted organic naval air protection on account of the threat from British Wildebeests! Attached to the IJN were the Special Naval Landing Forces (SNLF), which were intended to conduct diversionary attacks to the south of Hong Kong Island, drawing British attention away from the real thrust of the land invasion. Niimi also asked for the destroyers IJN *Wakaba* and *Yugure* on account of the threat from the three British destroyers, but his request was not granted.

The IJAF contributed the 1st Air Brigade under Col. Habu Hideharu with the 45th Air Regiment at its core consisting of 34 x Ki-32 Kawasaki (Type 98) 'Mary' light bombers[1]. This force was made up of a combination of units and planes amassed from airfields as far afield as Beijing, Shanghai, Taiwan and Qiqihar (Manchuria) that were all assembled in Baiyun Aerodrome in Guangzhou on 7 December 1941. Attached to the 1st Air Brigade was the 10th Independent Sqn., led by Captain Takatsuki Akira, 13 x Ki-27 Nakajima (Type 97) 'Nate' fighters, 3 x Ki-15 Mitsubishi (Type 97) 'Babs' command reconnaissance planes from the 18th Independent Reconnaissance Sqn. and the 44th Independent Sqn. with 6 x Ki-36 Tachikawa (Type-98) 'Ida' observation planes.

Years before the actual invasion, the Japanese planted moles and sleeper agents in Hong Kong, laboriously collecting information and mapping key military installations. Such was the efficiency of these intelligence networks that the invasion maps carried by IJA officers were actually Hong Kong Government or British military maps, overprinted with Japanese notes and interpretations! Senior British officers arriving at the POW camp were surprised to see that their regular barber at the Peninsula Hotel, the premier hotel in Hong Kong, was in fact a lieutenant-commander in the IJN, who had been taking advantage of the informal atmosphere at the barber's to gather valuable information about the status of British forces. The Japanese planted spies everywhere – the garrison tailor and barber were also both spies! The Japanese were able to be extremely accurate with their artillery and bombing as a direct result of this groundwork. They also made use of gangsters in both Hong Kong and Guangdong,[2] buying their loyalty and supplying them with weapons, so that they acted as auxiliaries to support the invasion.

---

1   On 8 December they were carrying 6 x 50kg bombs each.
2   'Chinese People's Self-Administration National Group Army', approximately 12,000 strong with 200 junks.

ORDERS OF BATTLE

BRITISH ORDER OF BATTLE, 8 DECEMBER 1941

Garrison Commander: Maj. Gen. C. M. Maltby CB MC

KOWLOON INFANTRY BRIGADE (KIB), COMMANDER: BRIGADIER B. C. WALLIS:

2nd Battalion, The Royal Scots: Lt. Col. S. E. H. E. White MC (left flank of Gin Drinkers Line including Shing Mun Redoubt and Golden Hill, later WIB)

2nd Battalion, 14th Punjab Regiment: Lt. Col. G. R. Kidd (centre of Gin Drinkers Line around Shatin area, less C Coy under Maj. C. E. Gray as Covering Force, New Territories)

5th Battalion, 7th Rajput Regiment: Lt. Col. J. Cadogan-Rawlinson (right flank of Gin Drinkers Line)

1 Coy HKVDC: Capt. A. H. Penn (Kai-Tak Airport Guard, in reserve for Gin Drinkers Line, one platoon with Bren carriers patrolling Castle Peak Road, withdrawal to Taitam Valley)

Engineer Coy HKVDC: Maj. J. H. Bottomley (Covering Force New Territories, Demolition, later withdrawal to Taihang area (near today's HK Stadium), Hong Kong)

Armoured Car Platoon HKVDC: Lt. M. G. Caruthers (Covering Force New Territories, later withdrawal to HQ West Brigade, Hong Kong)

Recce Platoon HKVDC: Lt. R. D. Edwards (Covering Force New Territories)

1 Mountain Battery, 1st Hong Kong Regiment HKSRA: Capt. (Temp. Maj.) E. W. De-Hunt (3.7in.) (Custom Pass, Kowloon – today the start of Clear Water Bay Road, Fei Ngo Shan)

2 Mountain Battery, 1st Hong Kong Regiment HKSRA: Maj. J. P. Crowe (3.7in. and 4in.) (Initially at Filters, New Territories, today just south of Kowloon Reservoir by Taipo Road, later withdrawn to Hong Kong: Stanley Gap)

25 Medium Battery, 1st Hong Kong Regiment HKSRA: Maj. W. Temple (6in.) (Polo Ground, Kowloon, today known as Tai Hang Tung Sports Ground)

HONG KONG INFANTRY BRIGADE (HKIB), COMMANDER: BRIGADIER J. K. LAWSON MC

1st Battalion, The Middlesex (machine-gun) Regiment: Lt. Col. H. W. M. Stewart OBE MC (located in 72 bunkers dotted around Hong Kong Island, operationally under the command of local units in the area where they were stationed)

The Royal Rifles of Canada: Lt. Col. W. J. Home (eastern section of the northern shores of Hong Kong, from Lyemun in the north-east to D'Aguilier Point on the east to Taitam and ending at Stanley village in the south-east of Hong Kong) (under command of C Coy Royal Rifles of Canada were HKVDC's No. 2 (Scottish) Machine Gun Coy, located Sheko to Cape Collinson, Hong Kong)

The Winnipeg Grenadiers: Lt. Col. J. L. R. Sutcliffe (western section of the northern shores of Hong Kong, stretching to Pokfulam in the west to Aberdeen in the south-west of the island and ending on the eastern side of Repulse Bay, south of Hong Kong) (D Coy: Wongneichong Gap under command of Brigade HQ as Brigade Reserve and Brigade Protection)

HKVDC: Col. H. B. Rose MC

3 (Eurasian) Machine Gun Coy: Maj. E. G. Stewart DSO (Stonecutter Island, later withdrawn to Jardine's Lookout Hong Kong)

4 (Chinese) Coy: Capt. R. K. Valentine (Hong Kong: Victoria Gap and Mt Kellett)

5 (Portuguese) Machine Gun Coy: Capt. C. A. D'Almada e Castro (Hong Kong: Mt Davis)

6 (Portuguese) Anti-aircraft Coy: Capt. H. A. de B. Botelho (Lewis guns – north shores of Hong Kong)

7 Coy: Maj. J. G. B. Dewar (Hong Kong: Magazine Gap Wanchai, Middle Gap)

Motor Machine Gun Platoon: Capt. J. Way

1st Independent Platoon: Lt. C. J. Norman (Hong Kong: Stanley)

2nd Home Guard Platoon (Hughsiliers): Maj. J. J. Patterson (Hong Kong Island North Shore, North Point power station)

Field Ambulance: Lt. Col. L. T. Ride (distributed around Hong Kong Island)

FORTRESS COMMAND: MAJ. GEN. C. M. MALTBY CB MC

Garrison RA – Commander: Brigadier T. McCleod

8th Coastal Regiment, RA: Lt. Col. S. Shaw MC (Coastal Defences: Eastern Command)

12th Coastal Battery: Maj. W. M. Stevenson (3 x 9.2in.) (Hong Kong: Stanley)

30th Coastal Battery: Maj. C. R. Templer (2 x 9.2in.) (Hong Kong: Bokhara Fort)

36th Coastal Battery: Capt. (Temp. Maj.) W. N. J. Pitt (2 x 6in. at each location) (Hong Kong: Collinson Fort, Chung Hom Kok Fort)

12th Coastal Regiment, RA: Maj. (Temp. Col.) R. L. J. Penfold (Coastal Defences: Western Command)

24th Coastal Battery: Capt. (Temp. Maj.) E. W. S. Anderson (3 x 9.2in.) (Hong Kong: Mt Davis)

26th Coastal Battery: Lt. (Temp. Maj.) A. O. G. Mills (3 x 6in.) (Stonecutters Island, Hong Kong: Jubilee Fort)

5th Heavy Anti-aircraft Regiment RA: Lt. Col. F. D. Field

7th Anti-aircraft Battery: Maj. W. A. C. H. Morgan (Hong Kong: West Bay, Wongneichong, Saiwan Fort)

17th Heavy Anti-aircraft Battery: Capt. (Temp. Maj.) A. R. Colquhoun (Hong Kong: Pinewood, Mt Davis, Brick Hill, Waterfall Bay)

18th Light Anti-aircraft Battery: Capt. (Temp. Maj.) J. C. Rochfort-Boyd (Lewis guns and Bofors) (Hong Kong: Stanley, Cape D'Aguilar Fort, Albany Road)

HKVDC (under command of Fortress RA)

1st Battery: Capt. G. F. Rees (2 x 4in.) (Coastal Defences: Eastern Command) (Hong Kong: Cape D'Aguilar Fort)

2nd Battery: Lt. (Temp. Capt.) D. J. S. Crozier (2 x 6in.)
(Coastal Defences: Eastern Command) (Hong Kong:
Bluff Head Fort, Stanley)

3rd Battery: Capt. C. W. L. Cole (2 x 4in.) (Coastal Defences:
Eastern Command, Hong Kong: Belcher's Fort)

4th Battery: Lt. K. M. A. Barnett (2 x 6in.) (Hong Kong:
Pakshawan Fort, Lyemun)

5th Anti-aircraft Battery: Capt. L. Goldman (3in.)
(Hong Kong: Saiwan Hill Fort)

1st Hong Kong Regiment, HKSRA: Maj. (Temp. Lt. Col.) J. C. Yale

3 Medium Battery: Capt. (Temp. Maj.) H. L. Duncan (6in.)
(Hong Kong: Mt Parker, Siu Wan Hill Fort)

4 Medium Battery: Maj. G. E. S. Proes (6in.)
(Hong Kong: Mt Gough, Mt Austin)

25 Medium Battery: Maj. W. T. Temple (6in.)
(Hong Kong Island: Stanley Gap, Jockey Club Stables)

965 Battery RA: Maj. B. T. C. Forrester (4.7in. and 6in., 2- and
18-pdr) (Hong Kong: Belchers Upper, Belchers Lower, Repulse
Bay, Taitam Bay, Stanley, Promontory, Island Bay, Deep Water,
Tai Ho Wan)

Garrison RE: Lt. Col. R. G. Lamb

22nd Fortress Company RE: Maj. D. C. E. Grose
(elements detached to Covering Force New Territories,
the rest in Fortress HQ Hong Kong)

40th Fortress Company RE: Maj. D. I. M. Murray (Harbour)

Others miscellaneous

Hong Kong Chinese Regiment: Maj. H. W. A. Mayer

Z Force: F. W. Kendal (SOE/Force 163)

**ROYAL NAVY, COMMANDER: CAPT. A. C. COLLINSON RN
(1,300, WITH 300 BEING INDIAN AND CHINESE)**

**2nd MTB flotilla, Commander: Lt. Cdr. G. H. Gandy RN
(Aberdeen)**

MTB *7*: Lt. R. R. W. Ashby DSC HKRNVR

MTB *8*: Lt. L. D. Kilbee HKRNVR

MTB *9*: Lt. A. Kennedy RNVR

MTB *10*: Lt. Cdr. G. H. Gandy RN

MTB *11*: Lt. C. J. Collingwood DSO RN

MTB *12*: Sub-Lt. J. B. Colls HKRNVR

MTB *26*: Lt. D. W. Wagstaff HKRNVR

MTB *27*: Lt. T. M. Parsons HKRNVR

Shallow-draught river gunboats

HMS *Cicala*: Lt. Cdr. J. C. Boldero RN (sunk by air strikes and
combined gunnery of IJN *Isuzu*, *Ikazuchi* and *Inazuma*)

HMS *Tern*: Lt. J. Douglas RN (scuttled)

HMS *Moth*: Lt. Cdr. R. C. Creer
(refitting 8 December 1941, fought as infantry)

HMS *Robin*: Cdr. H. M. Montague OBE RN
(damaged by IJN *Isuzu*, *Ikazuchi* and *Inazuma*, then scuttled)

S-class destroyers

HMS *Thracian*: Lt. Cdr. A. L. Pears RN (crew fought as infantry)

HMS *Thanet*, *Scout*: left for Singapore 2130hrs 8 December 1941

Arabis-class sloop HKRNVR drill ship: HMS *Cornflower*: Lt. Cdr. R.
J. D. Vernall HKRNVR

Fleet Air Arm, Commander: Lt. P. J. Milner-Barry RN

2 x Supermarine Walrus seaplanes
(1 x Walrus escaped 8 December 1941)

**Assortment of tugs, boom defence vessels and minelayers,
among which were:**

HMS *Redstart*: minelayer (scuttled)

HMS *Barlight*: minelayer (scuttled, but raised by Japanese as
Netlayer 101, sunk in Saipan 1944)

APV *Algate*: barrage/gate vessels (scuttled)

APV *Frosty*

APV *Han Wo* (scuttled)

APV *Indira*

APV *Margaret*

APV *Minnie*

APV *Perla*

APV *Poseidon*

APV *Shun Wo*

APV *St. Aubin*

APV *St. Sampson*

APV *Watergate* barrage/gate vessels (scuttled)

RFA *Ebonol* oiler (scuttled)

Hong Kong Dockyard Defence Corps: Maj. D. Campbell RM

Royal Marine Troop HMS *Tamar*: Col. R. G. Giles RM
(47 all ranks)

**ROYAL AIR FORCE, COMMANDER:
WNG. CDR. H. G. SULLIVAN**

2 x Vickers Wildebeest torpedo/light bombers
(1 x Wildebeest escaped 8 December 1941)

HKVDC flight

1 x Avro 621 Tutor, 2 x Hornet Moths, 2 x Cadet biplanes.

JAPANESE ORDER OF BATTLE, 8 DECEMBER 1941

**23RD ARMY: LT. GEN. SAKAI TAKASHI, CHIEF OF STAFF:
MAJ. GEN. KURIBAYASHI TADAMICHI, DEPUTY CHIEF
OF STAFF: MAJ. GEN. HIGUCHI KEISHICHIRO.**

**38th Division (NE of Shenzhen City, Shawan Town): Lt.
Gen. Sano Tadayoshi. Total divisional strength is 23,228.
Commander of Divisional Infantry (East of Shenzhen City,
Huangbei Ling): Maj. Gen. Ito Takeo.**

228th Infantry Regiment (Eastern shores Pearl River, Shajing,
Xi Xiang): Col. Doi Teihichi

1/228th: Maj. Hayakawa Kikuo

2/228th: Maj. Takeyoshi Inagaki

3/228th: Maj. Nishiyama Haruja

229th Infantry Regiment (NE of Shenzhen City, Heng Gang
Market): Col. Tanaka Ryosaburo

1/229th: Maj. Orita Sugura

2/229th: Maj. Sato Giichi

3/229th (Sha Tau Kok): Capt. Kojima

230th Infantry Regiment (North of Shenzhen City, Buji Town): Col. Shoji Toshishige

1/230th (West of Shenzhen City, Nantou District): Maj. Seki Eiji

2/230th: Maj. Takizawa Kanpei

3/230th: Maj. Ooneda Anpei

Divisional artillery

38th Mountain Artillery Regiment: Col. Kanki Takeyoshi (28 x Type 41 75mm mountain gun)

21st Mortar Battalion

10th Independent Mountain Artillery Regiment: Col. Sawamoto Rikichiro (24 x Type 41 75mm mountain gun)

20th Independent Mountain Artillery Battalion: Lt. Col. Kajimatsu Jiro (9 x Type 34 (Bofors) 75mm mountain guns)

2nd Independent Rapid Fire Artillery Battalion: Lt. Col. Ohno Takeo (18 x 37mm QF/anti-tank gun)

5th Independent Rapid Fire Artillery Battalion: Maj. Aoki Jiro (2 x 37mm QF/anti-tank gun)

Divisional engineers and Logistics

38th Logistic Regiment: Lt. Col. Yabuta Shuichi

38th Engineers Regiment: Lt. Col. Iwabuchi Tsuneo

19th Independent Engineer Regiment: Lt. Col. Inukai Shojiro

20th Independent Engineer Regiment: Col. Suzukawa Kiyoshi

2nd Coy of 14th Independent Engineering Regiment: Maj. Kusagi Eiichi

1st & 2nd River Crossing Material Company of 9th Division

Other divisional support

Armour Squadron: Capt. Atami Juro[3] (16 x tankettes?)

3rd Transport Regiment: Lt. Col. Kobayashi Otokazu (8-ton tractors x 18, 13-ton tractors x 14)

Three companies of 3rd Transport Regiment

Attached are 19th, 20th and 21st Independent Transport Company

One-third of the medical unit from 51st Division: Col. Hattori Otokazu

Two radio signal platoons and one wire signal platoon

Ordnance team: Capt. Koide Sadaharu

5th Field Chemical Company: Capt. Suzuki Magosaburo

18th Field Chemical Company: Lt. Morimoto Isao

Veterinary: Vet. Maj. Hayashi Jiro

1st Field Hospital: Dr. Maj. Suzuki Toshimi

2nd Field Hospital: Dr. Maj. Ito Takuzo

Field Pigeon Carrier Company (68 Pigeons)

South China MP Platoon: Maj. Noma Kennosuke

66th Infantry Regiment (less 1 Coy): Col. Araki, Katsutoshi. Attached from 51st Div., 23rd Army. All ranks: 5,892 with

Additional artillery support:

1st Heavy Artillery Regiment: Maj. Gen. Kitashima Kineo

1st Battalion: Col. Hayakawa Yoshimasa (8 x Type-45 240mm/9in. howitzer)

2nd Battalion Independent Heavy Artillery: Maj. Kanemaru Kiyotoshi (8 x Type-89, 150mm howitzer)

3rd Battalion Independent Heavy Artillery: Lt. Col. Nukina Hitomi (8 x Type-89, 150mm howitzer)

14th Heavy Field Artillery Regiment: Col. Sato Takeaki (6 x Type-4, 150mm howitzer)

2nd Independent Mortar Battalion: Maj. Namimatsu Teiichi (12 or 15 x Type-89 or Type-97 15cm mortar)

23rd Army Air Unit, 1st Air Group: Col. Habu Hideharu (all ranks 1,300)

45th Air Regiment: Col. H. Tsuchio, (34[4] x Ki-32) Kawasaki (Type-98) 'Mary' light bombers (Guangzhou)

10th Independent Air Squadron: Maj. Takatsuki Akira, (13[5] x Ki-27) Nakajima (Type-97) 'Nate' fighters

18th Independent Air Squadron: Capt. Kobayashi Minoru, (3 x Ki-15) Mitsubishi (Type 97) 'Babs' command recce plane

44th Independent Squadron: Capt. Naito Yoshio, (6 x Ki-36) Tachikawa (Type-98) 'Ida' army cooperation plane, (Guangzhou)

47th Air-Field Battalion: Maj. Uemura Sadayu

67th Air-Field Company of 67th Air Field Battalion: Capt. Kodama Nobunaga

Element of 57th Air-Field Company: 2nd Lt. Makita Mitsuhiro

IJN ELEMENT: 2ND CHINA FLEET, COMMANDER: VICE ADMIRAL NIIMI MASAICHI, CHIEF OF STAFF BRIGADIER YASUBA YASUO

Bombardment Group

IJN *Isuzu* light cruiser (Flagship): 15 Squadron, Guangzhou

IJN *Tsuga*: destroyer

IJN *Ikazuchi*: destroyer: 6 Division, 1st Fleet, Magong/Makung (Mako) Taiwan

IJN *Inazuma*: destroyer: 6 Division, 1st Fleet, Magong/Makung (Mako) Taiwan

IJN *Wakaba*: destroyer

IJN *Yugure*: destroyer

IJN *Kasasagi*: MTB, 15 Squadron, Guangzhou

IJN *Hiyodori*: MTB, China Theatre Fleet, Shanghai

IJN *Kari*: MTB, Torpedo Boat Squadron, Guangzhou

IJN *Kiji*: MTB, Torpedo Boat Squadron, Guangzhou

IJA *Tosho Maru*: armed cargo ship

IJN *Kamikawa Maru*: seaplane tender with 2 x Kawanishi E7K (Type 94) 'Alf' Seaplanes and 3 x Yokosuka B3Y (Type 92) torpedo attack planes (IJN Naval aviation 200 all ranks)

---

3 Type 94 (sometimes known as Type 92, 1932) tankettes were used in the battle of Hong Kong

4 Only 29 participated in the battle of Hong Kong. The regiment was originally based in Manchuria, NE China, and flew down especially to Guangzhou.

5 Only nine participated in the operation; one crashed en route from Manchuria where it was stationed.

Attack Group

IJN *Uiji*: gunboat (Force Flagship) Shanghai, detached to
Guangzhou

IJN *Hashidate*: gunboat, 15 Squadron, Guangzhou

IJN *Saga*: gunboat, 15 Squadron, Guangzhou

IJA *Arashiyama Maru*: armed cargo ship

IJA *Tsukushi Maru*: armed cargo ship

IJA *Asashi Maru*: armed cargo ship

IJA *Momo Maru*: armed cargo ship

IJN *Ryujin Maru*: armed cargo ship

IJN *Choun Maru* No. 7: auxiliary patrol boat / minesweeper

IJA *Shinsei Maru*: transporter

IJN *Sozan Maru*: auxiliary minelayer, Guangzhou

IJN *Azuchi Maru*: ammunition transport ship

San Luis Maru: auxiliary oiler

IJN *Shinko Maru*: minelayer, 14 Gunboat Division, Shanghai

IJN *Toen Maru*: fleet oiler, China Theatre Fleet Supply Unit,
Sasebo Japan

OPPOSING PLANS

BRITISH PLANS

Japan became a concern to Britain with the end of the Anglo-Japanese Alliance in the 1920s, and the subsequent Japanese invasion of China saw the relationship worsen. As the Sino-Japanese War deepened, the threat to British interest in the Far East increased, even to the point that the Japanese openly attacked Western commercial and military shipping, such as HMS *Ladybird*. However the British Government continued to be ambivalent towards Japan and any measures it took were weak and ineffective.

Although from a diplomatic standpoint Britain continued to take a soft line with Japan, from a military point of view Britain was worried. In the 1930s the largest and most prosperous British assets in the Far East were Singapore and Malaya and as such they were heavily defended. However, successive studies have all concluded that Hong Kong could not be defended effectively and the British Government never maintained the level of troops that was deemed necessary to protect it. Nevertheless, the British Government initiated the Hong Kong Defence Scheme 1936. The aim of the 1936 defence scheme focused on transforming Hong Kong Island into a fortress with light defences and delaying positions in Kowloon and the New Territories. The task of the Hong Kong Garrison was to 'defend the Colony from external attack and deny the use of the harbour and the dry dock to the enemy'. The strategy was to hold Hong Kong Island as a fortress and wait for rescue by the British fleet. It was therefore essential that Hong Kong should protect its harbour as its top priority. The Japanese were seen to be the main threat to Hong Kong and the military strategists deemed that the main avenue of attack would be by sea and not by land.

Bren carriers on manoeuvres somewhere in the New Territories on the mainland. This type of grassy, hilly terrain is typical of much of the New Territories, where much of the initial fighting occurred. Command of the high ground is vital to any military operation. (IWM)

26

To attack Hong Kong by sea the IJN would have to navigate five layers of defences: first naval mines with indicator nets and anti-submarine booms; next, the coastal guns; and if the former two layers of defence were penetrated, beach defences consisting of a series of pillboxes, wires and landmines; on the island, high on the hills, infantry strongpoints to defend against localized landings and to stop penetration; and finally a reserve force to counter-attack and destroy any enemy landings.

In addition the 1936 plan called for extensive construction of bunkers, trenches and blocking positions across bottleneck approaches to Kowloon and a main line of defence, a mini Maginot-style line of trenches and pillboxes across the mountains north of Kowloon. The army component listed only three infantry battalions plus the local Hong Kong militia, the Hong Kong Volunteer Defence Corps (HKVDC), a regiment-plus sized unit of armoured cars, engineers, artillery, anti-aircraft guns and infantry, all to be organized into three elements: the mainland brigade, the island brigade and the garrison reserve. In the 1936 defence scheme the RAF was expected to be exceptionally strong with one reconnaissance squadron, one fighter-bomber squadron, two torpedo squadrons and one flight of air auxiliary spotter planes from the HKVDC. The navy consisted of a couple of destroyers, a flotilla of MTBs and gunboats, and assorted patrol craft.

These activities were further boosted when the IJA occupied Guangzhou, and Hong Kong was effectively surrounded. Limited conscription was introduced but applied to only non-Chinese males for service with the

This set of anti-shipping booms was laid at the eastern entrance of Victoria Harbour, close to where the Japanese landing on Hong Kong Island took place. Together with indicator loops and controlled minefields, they formed the core naval element of the 1936 Defence Scheme. (IWM)

The main landmark of Kowloon, Lion Rock Mountain. Looking north, the plain below is now Western Kowloon, today a middle-class area full of high-rise buildings. The Lion Rock forms a ridge of mountains that stretch east–west across the northern tip of Kowloon where the Gin Drinkers Line was situated. (NAM)

B Coy, 1st Battalion the Middlesex Regiment, somewhere in the New Territories, 1940. Note they are armed with Short Magazine Lee-Enfields. This picture was taken by Private Henry Chick of B Coy, 1 Middlesex, who died in the sinking of the *Lisbon Maru* in 1942. (NAM)

HKVDC. Local Chinese mainly served in non-combat roles such as ARPs, medical units etc. As a result of the increasing Japanese threat, the Hong Kong Garrison was boosted to four regular infantry regiments: two British (one medium machine-gun role) and two Indian. In support were two regiments of coastal artillery, one regiment-plus worth of field artillery as well as a regiment of anti-aircraft guns. The Royal Navy in Hong Kong consisted of the 2nd MTB flotilla with eight BPB[6] 60 MTBs *7, 8, 9, 10, 11* and *12* (60ft, 29 knots, twin torpedoes with eight Lewis guns) and MTB *26* and *27* (ex-Chinese Navy Kuai *1* and *2*, British Thornycroft 55ft CMB), four shallow-draught, flat-bottom river gunboats (HMS *Cicala*, *Tern*, *Moth*, and *Robin*) and four old World War I S-class destroyers HMS *Thracian*, *Thanet*, *Scout* and *Tenedos* (left in 1939 for Singapore) as well as a Navy sloop HMS *Cornflower* plus an assortment of tugs, boom defence vessels and minelayers. The Fleet Air Arm was represented by three Supermarine Walruses – single-engine reconnaissance amphibians co-located with the Air Force in Kai Tak Airport. The Royal Air Force was the weakest of the three services with only four Vickers Wildebeest torpedo/light bombers and a flight from the HKVDC consisting of a single Avro 621 Tutor, two Hornet Moths and two Cadet biplanes.

However, in the early years of World War II, Britain was preoccupied with national survival; it was unavoidable that little or no effort was placed on the defence of the Empire, especially far-flung outposts like Hong Kong. Not only were there no additional reinforcements, the outbreak of war in Europe resulted in many of the better soldiers being sent back there, with the less capable left in Hong Kong. Furthermore during years of peacetime garrison duties many had spent more time drinking cocktails and attending concert parties than honing their fighting skills.

Governor Sir Geoffrey Northcote lobbied London vigorously for a stern response to the continuous Japanese harassment – flying warplanes, sinking

6 British Power Boat Company – a maker of high-speed boats in Britain

The Hong Kong Chinese Regiment raised as a machine-gun battalion on 3 November 1941 with an establishment of six Chinese NCOs and 46 men, led by two British officers and three regular NCOs. By Christmas Day 1941, 31 of the original 57 members were killed or wounded, a 54 per cent casualty rate in three weeks. (IWM)

junks and fishing vessels, as well as the infiltration of Hong Kong by Taiwanese fifth columnists (Taiwan had become a Japanese colony in 1895). With his hands tied, in October 1940, the ailing Northcote recommended the withdrawal of the garrison 'in order to avoid the slaughter of civilians and the destruction of property which would follow a Japanese attack', knowing that in all practical respects Hong Kong was indefensible against a determined Japanese attack. However, London opposed this suggestion – 'such action, it was felt, would discourage China, encourage Japan and shake American faith in Britain.' A key and probably the most critical political consideration was the never-ending tussle between China and Britain over the sovereignty of Hong Kong. Ever since Hong Kong had been ceded to Britain in 1841, the British had feared that, if it was given up without a fight, it would be that much more difficult to reclaim it under British rule after the war. London felt that it was important to 'show Chiang Kai-shek [the leader of Nationalist China] the reality of our intention to hold the Island'.

However, London continued to avoid any request for extra troops. The request by Major-General A. E. Grasett DSO MC, GOC China, for reinforcement was flatly refused, the only help offered being from Indian or other colonial forces. In 1941 the newly appointed British GOC in the Far East, Air Chief Marshal Sir Robert Brooke-Popham again pressed his superiors to reinforce the garrison of Hong Kong. His request fell on deaf ears.

In July 1941 Grasett, a Canadian who had just retired from his appointment as GOC China, returned to Britain by way of Canada and, whilst in Canada, acting on his own initiative, called upon his former classmate Maj. Gen. Crerar, Chief of Canadian General Staff, and lobbied for reinforcement, arguing that the 'addition of two or more battalions to the forces then at Hong Kong would render the garrison strong enough to withstand for an extensive period of siege'. On 5 September 1941, shortly after reaching London, Grasett met with the British Chief of Staff and argued strongly for reinforcement, and suggested that Canada might supply the additional units to Hong Kong. The British chiefs were convinced and they persuaded the reluctant Churchill to change his mind. In the light of the looming Japanese threat, the defence of Malaysia/Singapore, the linchpin of the British Empire in the Far East, was boosted from nine battalions to 32 and the dispatch of two capital ships (HMS *Prince of Wales* and *Repulse*) to the area was seen to be enough of a deterrent to the Japanese against any 'inappropriate' action against British interests in the Far East, Hong Kong included.

The original Hong Kong war strategy was only to defend Hong Kong Island and deny the harbour to the enemy. A solitary battalion (the Punjabis) was to fight a series of delaying actions in the New Territories and conduct a short defence with three battalions on the Gin Drinkers Line to buy time to demolish stores, powerhouses, docks, wharves, clear food stocks, vital necessities, etc., on the mainland and then withdraw to Hong Kong Island and fight until relief arrived – either from Singapore or from the Americans in the Philippines.

The Gin Drinkers Line (a mini-Maginot Line) was located some 18km south of the Sino-Hong Kong border. The line was so named because it began to the west of Kowloon at a place called Gin Drinkers Bay. It stretched 17km across the hills of Kowloon to the eastern edge of the Kowloon Peninsula. The Gin Drinkers Line was expected to hold the Japanese for three weeks or more before the battalion retired to Hong Kong Island to hold on as long as it could while waiting for relief and while the mainland was evacuated. To defend Hong Kong effectively, the 1937 war plan estimated that it would require four battalions to fight an effective delaying action and up to seven to defend the Gin Drinkers Line, not to mention back-up from an adequate air force plus a blockade-busting navy. However, with one army brigade available and a virtually non-existent air force, the plan to hold the Gin Drinkers Line and the defence of the mainland was soon abandoned and the defence facilities remained incomplete and wasted away in the tropical heat.

The local Chinese were generally not engaged in any of the war preparations nor integrated into any of the war plans until very late. The biggest contingent was a group of volunteer Chinese that served with the HKVDC. On the regular army side, 150 Chinese were recruited in mid-1941 for service with the 5th Anti-aircraft Regiment. The Hong Kong Chinese Regiment, formed only on 3 November 1941, with officers borrowed from the British and Indian Regiments and 52 Chinese junior NCOs and other ranks that were barely trained. There was a troop of Royal Engineers staffed entirely by Chinese and a handful saw service with the Royal Navy and in the Dockyard Defence

Part-time soldiers of the HKVDC in training. Like all Territorials, training took place after work or during leisure time. Soldiering in the pre-World War II period was segregated along racial lines and all the young men in the picture are Eurasian; most probably they are soldiers of the No. 3 Eurasian Coy. (IWM)

Corps. However, in the auxiliary services such as the ARPs, auxiliary police, nursing services, St John Ambulance and fire service, the participation of Chinese was somewhat higher.

This unwillingness to engage the Chinese wholeheartedly in the defence of Hong Kong probably had to do with the general prevailing attitude of the time. Pre-war propaganda often ridiculed the Japanese as short-sighted and incompetent. The fighting ability of Japanese soldiers was played down; success in China was dismissed, as the Japanese had never encountered 'quality opposition'; furthermore the general consensus was that Japanese weapons were not up to European standards. In general the British were confident that if the colony was attacked, provided they had reinforcements, they could hold out indefinitely.

In September 1941, Hong Kong welcomed the news that two additional Canadian battalions were being made available to Hong Kong. Maltby immediately dusted off the pre-war plan of holding the Gin Drinkers Line. He devised a plan that called for three infantry battalions on the mainland (2 Royal Scots, 5/7 Rajputs and 2/14 Punjab, elements of HKVDC with support of four troops of the Hong Kong and Singapore Royal Artillery and the Coastal Artillery), and three infantry battalions (1 Middlesex, Royal Rifles of Canada and Winnipeg Grenadiers) reinforced by the bulk of the HKVDC holding Hong Kong Island. These were to be split into two brigades: the Island Brigade, named Hong Kong Infantry Brigade (HKIB) commanded by Brigadier Lawson of the newly arrived Canadian reinforcements and the mainland brigade, named Kowloon Infantry Brigade (KIB), commanded by Brigadier Wallis. The two Canadian regiments arrived in Hong Kong on 16 November 1941.

The Gin Drinkers Line was located in a very commanding position, perched on a range of mountains that stretched across the northern part of the Kowloon Peninsula. The line had certain inherent weaknesses. It had little depth and could be easily outflanked, two locations being particularly dangerous: Customs Pass and the gap between Golden Hill and Laichikok Peninsula (the area around Gin Drinkers Bay). Owing to the extensive front, each battalion's layout consisted of a line of platoon placements, the gaps between which were covered by fire by day and by patrols at night. One company from each battalion could be kept in reserve and it was normally located in a prepared position, covering the most dangerous

Because of concern about their loyalty in the event of conflict with China, Hong Kong Chinese were not recruited in large numbers until the 1930s, when threat of war with Japan became serious. By December 1941, 25 per cent of the Royal Engineers were local Chinese. Seen here are Hong Kong Chinese serving as regulars in the Royal Engineers. (IWM)

approaches. The reserve company of the centre battalion (2/14 Punjab) was employed initially as forward troops to cover the demolitions and to delay the enemy's initial advance.

The last-minute change of plan, to include a defensive force on the mainland at short notice, meant that many of the means of support such as communication lines, artillery and mortar registrations were not complete before the Japanese attacked. The lack of artillery shells and mortar bombs was another hindrance. For instance, in the worst

Battery command post of the HKSRA in 1941. The HKSRA was the largest colonial unit ever raised by Britain. It was essentially a British-officered, Indian Regular Artillery Regiment, recruited for service, as the name suggests, in Hong Kong and Singapore. (IWM)

case, the 2/14 Punjab had undergone one 3in. mortar practice session, of a few rounds only, but ammunition in any appreciable quantity did not arrive until November and then only 70 rounds per battalion, both for war and for practice. Hence these mortars were fired and registered for the first time in their battle positions and 12 hours later were in action against the enemy. For the 2in. mortar the situation was even worse. Not until the start of the battle did the troops receive any live bombs and consequently the first time they used this weapon was against the enemy! Because of the lack of transport, trucks or even mules, everything, including ammunition, had to be moved by hand and, on hilly terrain like Hong Kong, that would have been a test of endurance to say the least.

JAPANESE PLANS

On 6 November 1941 The Japanese Imperial Headquarters ordered its Commander-in-Chief China to prepare plans for the capture of Hong Kong. The 23rd Army of the China Southern Expeditionary Army Group under the command of Lt. Gen. Sakai Takashi with Maj. Gen. Kuribayashi Tadamichi as Chief of Staff was to form the core of the force and all preparations were to be complete by the end of November 1941. The aim of the plan, known as 'Operation C', was to 'capture Hong Kong within ten days'. Operation C was a relatively simple set of plans. First a blocking force was to prevent interference by the Chinese from the rear and secondly an invasion force was to lead the attack. The 23rd Army, consisting of four divisions plus a mixed brigade and two infantry regiments, was assigned the task of attacking Hong Kong. Of the four divisions only one, the 38th, played an active role in the invasion.

Disposition and movement of IJA forces prior to 8 December 1941

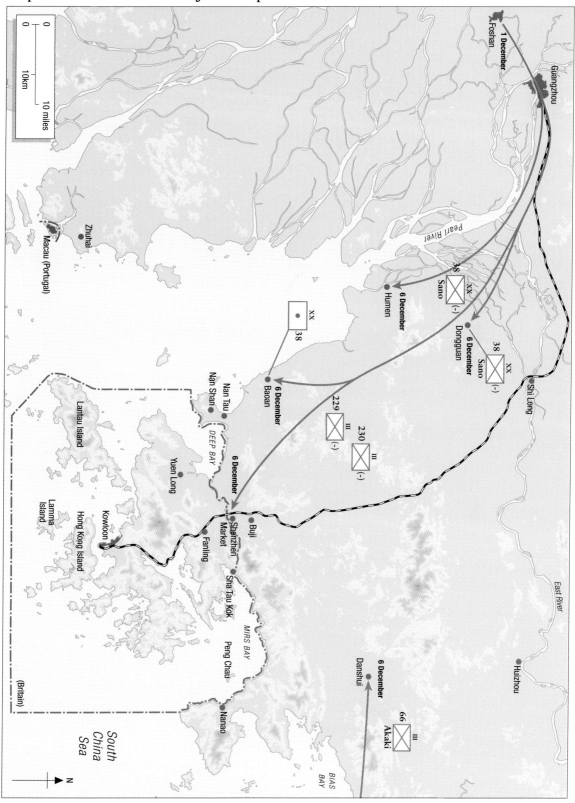

The attacking force was a combined arms effort; first there was a naval blockade and bombardment, combined with air attack on key installations, before a land invasion by elements of the 38th Division, consisting of 228th, 229th and 230th Regiments. They adopted a classic left, right and centre approach. The right force was to strike to the west, making a large hook curving right to clear the Castle Peak Road and strike at the vital point around the left flank of the Gin Drinkers Line around Laichikok Peninsula, while the centre force was to exploit the centre of the line, and the left force was to cross Tide Cove (Tolo Harbour) heading towards Kai Tak Airport and eastwards towards Devil Peak, a major battery position. The aim was to destroy the British on the mainland and force Hong Kong to surrender by intense bombardment. If the British continued to hold out, the invasion of the island would have only just begun.

Protecting the rear against the Chinese National Army of the 7th Military District and Communist Guerrillas and securing the assembly areas was the work of the 66th Regiment (normally part of the 51st Division, for the duration of the invasion, it was attached to 38th Division). The 66th was also responsible for occupying and securing the rear zones in the New Territories and Kowloon while the three spearhead regiments fought. This rearguard force was divided into columns known by the names of their commanders, Kitazawa, Kobayashi, Sato and Araki.

The IJA chose the closest point between Kowloon and Hong Kong Island, on the eastern end of the island around Lyemun Passage (at its narrowest, only 410m separate the mainland with Hong Kong Island). Once they had landed, they were to move rapidly inland to capture the vital point of Wongneichong Gap and then turn west and south to capture Victoria City and the rest of Hong Kong.

The naval element was divided into two parts, the Bombardment Group and the attack Group. Attached to the force were approximately 300 members of the Naval Infantry (SNLF). The IJAF contributed to the invasion with 56 light bombers and fighters of the First Air Brigade under Col. Habu Hideharu. The mission was to support the land-based troops by destroying the Royal Air Force and Royal Navy.

Sha Tau Kok village sits astride the Sino-Hong Kong border. The border bisects the main shopping street of Sha Tou Kok village, creating the effect of a mini-Berlin in the Cold War. Note the IJA soldier on the other side of the barbed wire. (IWM)

THE BATTLE

7–10 DECEMBER 1941

On Sunday 7 December, 700 members of 2 Royal Scots and the Middlesex Regiment were marching to St John's Cathedral for the church service. Major-General Maltby was reading a passage from the book of Matthew, when his aide de camp Lt. I. MacGregor brought him a message. On 5 December the HKVDC was already fully mobilized, but the bulk of Hong Kong had behaved as if nothing had happened; the Happy Valley racetrack recorded its highest attendance. As part of the invasion of Hong Kong the Japanese started to move their force into assembly areas as soon the orders were given for war on 1 December. However, the IJA did not have far to move; in the autumn of 1941, the 23rd Army was already stationed in the west of Guangzhou (Canton); some were as far as Foshan Town, while others were in Zhuhai, a town west of Hong Kong across the mouth of the Pearl River. In preparation for the invasion of Hong Kong, the 23rd Army moved to Humen (a town south-west of Guangzhou) and Shilong Town (just east of Guangzhou) and Guangzhou itself. The Japanese were seen landing at Mirs Bay on 4–5 December 1941 and the 228th Regiment moved into its staging area in Buji Town, now part of Shenzhen City; these movements were

Luo Hu (Luo Wu) Border Crossing in 1938, British and Sikh soldiers and policemen facing off the IJA in a tense stand-off. The railway bridge seen in the photo is still present at the Luo Hu border post, now no longer in service but preserved as a historical memorial. (Hong Kong Library)

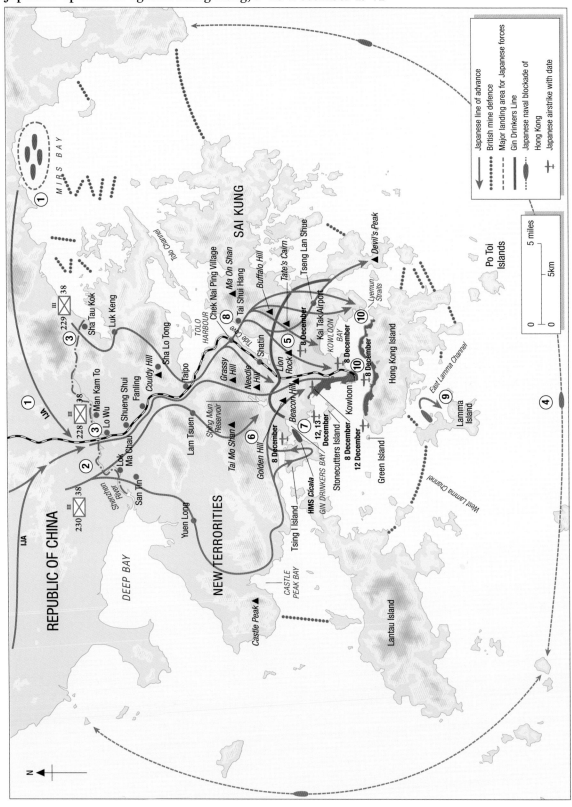

1. Japanese forces began landing in Mirs Bay on 4/5 December 1941. In preparation for the invasion of Hong Kong, the 23rd Army moved to Humen, Shi Long Town and Guangzhou itself. The 228th Regiment's assembly areas were in Buji Town in modern Shenzhen City. The 66th Regiment was responsible for rearguard operations and securing the assembly areas against the Chinese National Army and Communist Guerrillas.
2. The IJA Southern Expeditionary Army Group, 23rd Army, commanded by Lt. Gen. Sakai Takashi, was tasked with capturing Hong Kong. The invasion itself was codenamed Operation *C* and the 38th Division under Maj. Gen. Sano Tadayoshi led the invasion.
3. Sakai gave the order to launch the invasion at 0351hrs and the 230th, 229th and 228th Regiments crossed the Shenzhen River at 0600hrs on 8 December 1941. Initial objectives for the 228th Regiment were to cross Shenzhen River at Lok Ma Chau, Lo Wu and Man Kam To, passing Lam Tsuen Village to take the low ground at the southern foot of Grassy Hill/northern foot of Needle Hill. The 229th Regiment crossed the start line at Sha Tau Kok then went via Luk Keng to Sha Lo Tong and then to Chek Nai Ping village. They then were to cross Tide Cove landing at Tai Shui Hang, the objective for the following day was to take Buffalo Hill. The 230th Regiment was responsible for the west flank and was to split into two parts, one part was to reach the foot of Tai Mo Shan and another was to go west via Yuen Long and Castle Peak Bay to clear the west flank of British troops.
4. The light cruiser *Isuzu* was the flagship of the Hong Kong invasion fleet commanded by Vice-Admiral Niimi Masaichi of the Second China Expeditionary Fleet. The Naval invasion force included the 15th Escort Squadron, commanded by Vice-Admiral Hara Kiyoshi, with Torpedo Boat Division 1, Minesweeper Divisions 4 and 44. Seconded to the Second China Expeditionary fleet were the destroyer *Tsuga* and the auxiliary gun boat *Tosho Maru* from the China Area Fleet based in Shanghai as well as the destroyers *Ikazuchi* and *Inazuma* from Destroyer Division 6 of the First Fleet.
5. On 8 December 1941, IJAF planes left Guangzhou at 0720hrs for Hong Kong. At *c.*0800hrs 12 Ki-36s from the 45th Sentai, escorted by nine Ki-27s from the 10th Independent Chutai led by Captain Takatsuki Akira, attacked Kai Tak airport. All five of the token RAF aircraft stationed at Kai Tak were quickly damaged or destroyed, as were numerous light trainers and civilian cargo planes. In the harbour, Pan Am's visiting Sikorsky S-42B flying boat the 'Hong Kong Clipper' was bombed, set on fire and sunk. Japanese aircraft also attacked Shamshuipo Camp where the Winnipeg Grenadiers were based. The Taikoo and Kowloon Docks and city of Kowloon were also bombed.
6. 9/10 December: the Shing Mun Redoubt on the western flank of Gin Drinkers Line was breeched by 3/228th Regiment.
7. 10 December: HMS *Cicala* on station near Tsing I Island shelled the Japanese 230th Regiment. Troops on Castle Peak road are attacked by Japanese bombers.
8. The 229th Regiment was only able to cross Tide Cove on the afternoon of 10 December having been held up by delaying actions.
9. 11 December, morning: Japanese naval landing forces landed on Lamma Island and tried to cross the straits to Aberdeen Island but were driven off. British forces began to withdraw from Kowloon after the collapse of the Royal Scots' positions in and around the Shing Mun Reservoir area.
10. 12 December, dawn: advance IJA forces reached the southern tip of the Kowloon Peninsula. Japanese bombers dived on Mt Davis battery. The last of the British Forces were evacuated by the Navy from Devil's Peak on the 13th.

reported to Maltby, whereupon he hurriedly left the service and proceeded to issue an order for immediate stand-to. Despite the ominous signs, there were people within the military community that doubted the seriousness of the situation and the possibility of war, with talk of the 'astonishingly erroneous intelligence summary to the War Office'. This was at the same time that the IJN was massing just beyond Hong Kong waters.

The KIB consisted of 5/7 Rajputs at the centre, 2/14 Punjab in the east, and 2 Royal Scots in the west, with its C Coy under Maj. S. Burns forward, patrolling along Castle Peak Road all the way to Yuen Long. C Coy, 2/14 Punjab, was the Brigade screen and took up positions in the area of Shueng Shui and Taipo Market with four Bren carriers and two armoured cars of the HKVDC. With C Coy, 2/14 Punjab, were the engineers of the HKVDC and 22nd Fortress Company Royal Engineers. Under the command of the KIB were 1st and 2nd Bty. and the 25th Medium Bty. of the 1st Hong Kong Regiment, Hong Kong Singapore Royal Artillery.

The Canadians, initially part of the HKIB with the Winnipeg Grenadiers at Victoria City (today's Sheungwan and Western, on the north-west coastline of Hong Kong Island) and the Royal Rifles of Canada were based on the northern-eastern shores of Hong Kong Island from Saukiwan to Lyemun. HKIB HQ with Brigadier Lawson in command was located at the Wongneichong Gap in the centre of Hong Kong Island.

At 0355hrs local time on 8 December the code word 'Blossom Blossom' was given; 11 minutes later, Lt. Gen. Sakai gave his order to commence invasion. Some 50 minutes later, at 0445hrs Maj. Charles Boxer, formerly of the Lincolnshire Regiment, the senior intelligence officer and a fluent Japanese speaker, was woken by Radio Tokyo telling its citizens that war was imminent. Governor Young and Maj. Gen. Maltby were immediately informed.

A formation of Type 98 'Mary' bombers and 'Nate' fighters flying due west having just passed Kowloon Peninsula on 8 December 1941. The area from which smoke is bellowing is Shamshuipo, the location of the Canadian barracks. (Author's collection)

By 0500hrs Maj. Gray OC C Coy, and battalion second in command of the 2/14 Punjab, and the engineer company of the HKVDC under Maj. J. H. Bottomley successfully blew all forward demolition points. At 0645hrs the garrison was told that the British Empire and Japan were at war. Seventy-five minutes later an air-raid siren sounded and immediately clouds of smoke were seen rising from Kai-Tak Airport. In a matter of minutes, all the Wildebeest, Walruses, as well as the biplanes of the HKVDC and several civilian planes were left blazing. Luckily two Ju-52s of the Eurasia Corporation and one CNAC[7] T32 Condor escaped destruction. Attempts to disperse the aircraft were futile as no dispersal bays had been built because of a lack of funds. The Japanese then switched to secondary targets by dropping bombs on Shamshuipo Camp and the neighbouring police station. The Canadians largely escaped any large-scale casualties except for the signal platoon's Sgt. Routledge and Signalman Fairley. They became the first Canadian soldiers to be wounded in World War II. Despite the war, theatres, cinemas and restaurants were still functioning as if nothing had happened on Hong Kong Island!

The demolition proved to be no more than a minor irritant to the Japanese. No sooner had bridges been blown, than the Japanese had installed replacements. The Japanese were crossing into Hong Kong on three fronts; on the western route came the 230th Regiment with a two-battalion frontage, proceeding westwards towards Yuen Long and the Castle Peak area. The immediate objective was the bottom of the northern slope of Tai Mo Mountain (957m). In the centre was the 228th Regiment operating with two battalions forward. Their advance was to follow the Sheung Shui–Taipo–Kowloon road to reach the southern foot of Grassy Hill just north of the Shing Mun Redoubt. On the east came 229th Regiment. It crossed the border at Sha Tau Kok and by boat at Starling Inlet and proceeded towards Taipo via Sha Lo Tong before

7   China National Aviation Corporation

crossing Tide Cove to land at Tai Shui Hang village and then cross Ma On Mountain. Whenever the IJA encountered strongly defended localities, instead of fighting them, they simply bypassed these positions.

During the first day there were intermittent skirmishes all around the New Territories. The first encounter occurred at around 1300hrs, when the Punjabis gave the Japanese a bloody nose; later at 1830hrs the Punjabis again successfully ambushed and wiped out several platoons of Japanese, just past the causeway south of the market town of Taipo. These early successes were not limited to the regular army. Farther down the road the armoured cars and Bren carriers of the part-time HKVDC also wiped out another group of advancing Japanese. The reconnaissance platoon Bren carriers of the 2 Royal Scots made contact with elements of the 229th Regiment around Yuen Long. Despite these minor successes, the Japanese continued to advance, aided by stolen British maps as well as expert guidance from fifth columnists. By late afternoon on the 8th, to avoid being outflanked, the Punjabis had already withdrawn to a point close to Grassy Hill. The Gunners played an active role also, with 12th Bty. engaging an IJN destroyer and the IJA in Taipo, inflicting serious casualties.

At 2200hrs, farther south on the Taipo–Kowloon highway towards the town of Shatin, the rapidly advancing Japanese managed to catch the defenders by surprise and cut the fuse at one of the HKVDC's demolition points, but their jubilation was short lived; the HKVDC's engineers completed the back-up circuit and blew up the bridge along with the Japanese soldiers.

By the end of the first day, early on the 9th, orders were given for all mainland units to withdraw to the Gin Drinkers Line. The Punjabis were already at the head of Tide Cove at Shatin Wai and, although under pressure and continuous shelling, continued to hold for the next two days. The HKVDC were near Fotan, a village just south of Shatin. To plug the gap between the 2 Royal Scots and 2/14 Punjab, Maltby order the reserve company, D Coy, 5/7 Rajputs, under the command of Capt. H. R. Newtons to Smuggler's Ridge. The same day the armoured cars and Bren carriers of No. 1 Coy, HKVDC, were patrolling along Castle Peak Road and HMS *Cicala* was on patrol station by Castle Peak Bay having survived two air attacks. The IJN was already on station holding a blockade but somehow it still allowed HMS *Thanet* and *Scout* to slip anchor and escape to Singapore at around 2130hrs.

The surviving CNAC and Eurasia planes took off with VIP evacuees including Dr. Sun Yat-Sen's wife and her two equally famous sisters (the Soong sisters), Chinese Finance Minister H. H. Kung as well as Lt. Col. H. Owen-Hughes of the HKVDC, who was on a secret mission to coordinate with the Chinese Nationalist Army to come to aid Hong Kong by attacking the IJA from the rear.

LOSS OF THE SHING MUN REDOUBT

At around 1500hrs on the 9th, Col. Doi, CO of the 228th Regiment, was ahead of his two battalions on Needle Hill (532m), just north of Gin Drinkers Line. For the last two hours he had conducted reconnaissance on the main British defensive line. Although he could see no soldiers, he could see trenches and bunkers and to his surprise white clothes hanging on washing lines!

Japanese landing in Tide Cove (today named Tolo Harbour) on the first day of the battle of Hong Kong. Note the 'landing craft' in the background. These boats were part of the 1st and 2nd River Crossing Material Company attached to the 20th Independent Engineer Regiment. (Author's collection)

This clearly illustrated the lax and unprofessional nature of the 2 Royal Scots at this location. Suddenly heavy fog fell on the area and visibility dropped to less than 20m and heavy rain prevented further reconnaissance.

Doi could sense the unique opportunity and wanted to attack immediately but the weather caused him to lose touch with his battalions. Another problem he faced was that the Shing Mun Redoubt was not within his regimental boundary; attacking it was not his responsibility! Furthermore, when Doi's battalions did arrive, the supporting artillery was not available, as they were held back by the demolition on the Taipo Road.

Despite the possibility of serious punishment, Doi decided to attack. He ordered his 2/228th with about 800 men under Maj. Takeyoshi Inagaki to go left (east) to reconnoitre the route and preparation area as well as the enemy locations, while the 3/228th was to spearhead the attack. Major Nishiyana Haruja, CO of the 3/228th ordered Lt. Wakabayashi Touiti OC 10th Coy and Lt. Kasugai Yoshitaro[8] OC 9th Coy with 150 volunteers to lead the attack.

The Shing Mun Redoubt consisted of five pillboxes: 400, 401a, 401b, 402 and 403 and an artillery OP (341m) that doubled as the redoubt HQ. These were all built of reinforced concrete with steel doors and protectors for firing loopholes. Connected to the pillboxes and OPs was a system of underground concrete tunnels punctuated by open top concrete trenches; each tunnel was named after a famous London landmark (Piccadilly, Haymarket, etc.). These pillboxes were situated on the small knolls, described by the Japanese as points 255m (Pillbox 401b) and 341m (OP), on the south-east side of the reservoir across Jubilee Dam, at the time the tallest dam in the British Empire. The majority of the redoubt was, in fact, situated at the lower western reach of Smuggler's Ridge, in the vicinity of 381m spot-height (the British military map reference).

In defence of the redoubt was A Coy, 2 Royal Scots, under the command of Capt. C. R. Jones. Attached to A Coy was a FOO party from 2 Bty. 1st Hong Kong Regiment HKSRA, under the command of Lt. L. C. Wilcox; with him were two British and two Indian other ranks. A Coy, 2 Royal Scots, at Shing Mun was seriously undermanned. In the Coy HQ were one officer and nine other ranks. Under A Coy was effectively only one platoon, 8th Platoon,

8   Originally it was not Lt. Kasugai's 9th Coy leading the attack; a nameless company commander had been sacked, having been accused of being 'too noisy' during battle preparation.

commanded by 2nd Lt. J. S. R. Thompson with platoon Sgt. Robb and 25 men. In total, three officers and 39 men were facing an attacking force of 150 Japanese with a further battalion and a half, close to 1,500 troops, in reserve. In keeping with brigade orders, Lt. Col. White, CO of 2 Royal Scots, impressed on all ranks that the concrete defence works were to be used only by the Vickers medium machine-gun team and for storage and protection against artillery and mortar fire. The need for sustained patrol activities was stressed; critically, no mines could be spared for the redoubt.

On the night of the 9th about half of the defenders were inside the OP. The remaining half were said to have been deployed at locations in or near pillboxes 401b and 402. The 2 Royal Scots Battalion HQ was at 'Skeet Ground' on the south-west side of the redoubt, just east of Castle Peak Road below Smuggler's Ridge. On the south-east of the redoubt, along the eastern end of Smuggler's Ridge, was D Coy, 5/7 Rajputs, commanded by Capt. H. R. Newton, with interlocking firing arcs over Shing Mun Valley and orders to patrol the area around Needle Hill and Jubilee Dam.

By 1800hrs on the 9th the main body of the Japanese force was only some 500m off the dam, conducting battle preparations. At around 2000hrs, 2nd Lt. Thompson with a group of nine soldiers went on patrol. His orders, given by Lt. Col. White himself, were to 'patrol to the north, to check on any enemy on the southern slope of Needle Hill and in the Shing Mun Valley, and his patrol should then return via D Coy, 5/7 Rajputs'. Thompson returned at 2220hrs, having spent some time with Capt. Newton, incredibly after two and a half hours of patrolling, failing to detect either the 150-strong attacking force or any signs of the two battalions of Japanese nearby (even though the closest group of Japanese was only 500m away[9]). Meanwhile the attacking force led by Lt. Kasugai had crossed the Jubilee Dam, gone past the unmanned bungalow Post X at the south-west end of the dam, all without being detected, and by 2130hrs had assembled below Point 255 (Pillbox 401b). By 2200hrs 2nd Lt. Yamada Shoji of the 1st Platoon, 9th Company, had already cut through two lines of barbed wire. Seeing their progress, Maj. Nishiyana dispatched 10th Coy under Lt. Wakabayashi to join the attack. Lieutenant Wakabayashi immediately ordered his 1st Platoon to begin to move to attack Pillbox 403. H-Hour was intended to be at 2300hrs and, almost at the same time, L/Cpl. J. Laird at Pillbox 410b heard noises in the bushes and immediately opened fire. The Japanese responded with grenades and gunfire and rushed towards pillboxes 401a and 401b. One group of Japanese entered the tunnel and another group remained above ground and hurled grenades into the tunnel air vents. Corporal Campbell in the vicinity of Pillbox 402, heard the commotion, turned his Vickers machine gun and fired towards Pillbox 401. Members of the 3/228th HQ were caught in the open and suffered casualties. The attack alerted Sgt. Robb and he immediately gathered

The Shing Mun Redoubt. The picture on the wall is Lt. Wakabayashi Touiti OC 10th Coy, 3/228th Regiment. The vertical writing on the left is carved on the wall of the redoubt – 'Captured by Wakabayashi's unit'. This is located on the entrance of Shaftesbury Avenue on the map on page 44–45. (Author's collection)

9 According to the Royal Scots archive: 'It seems beyond doubt, in view of the short time that had elapsed, that Thompson did not patrol to Shing Mun River or Needle Hill.'

Captain Cyril. R. 'Potato' Jones of A Coy, 2 Royal Scots, seen in a Japanese newsreel while marching to captivity on 25 December 1941. Jones was actually commissioned into the East Lancashire Regiment in 1926 and became a temporary major on 23 November 1940. (Author's collection)

a force to counter-attack. Of the 13 that counter-attacked five became casualties (L/Cpl. Bankier, Ptes. Basnett, Coyle, Casey and Jardine). As Robb withdrew, Casey was killed and the Japanese managed to capture the party except for Pte. Jardine, who managed to escape. The battle also alerted Wilcox and he immediately called down a fire mission with both 4.5in. and 6in. guns from the HKSRA. Without strong back-up and strong leadership, about four members of the Royal Scots and an Indian sentry located in the northernmost posts abandoned their forward positions and withdrew southwards to take shelter in the OP.

The news of the attack was reported to brigade HQ and Jones was ordered by Wallis to lead the counter-attack to evict the enemy; Jones delegated Thompson to do the job but, as he tried to leave the OP, he found that it was locked from the outside. By this time 2nd Lt. Mochizuki and his platoon (10th Coy) had infiltrated through open trenches and began attacking the OP from the top, trying to gain entrance via the hatches.

How did this debacle come about? Just before the attack began, 2nd Lt. Thompson received a civilian at the OP, at the request of F. W. Kendal of Z Force, under the command of SOE/Force 163 Singapore (which carried out sabotage work behind enemy lines). Private Wylie was dispatched, taking the key to the OP from Lance Naik Kishan Singh, an Indian soldier from the HKSRA and, on exiting, locked the OP gate from the outside. Therefore at the most critical moment, the three officers were literally 'locked out'[10] of the battle. Sometime after 0100hrs on the 10th, Kendal reached the vicinity of the redoubt and found L/Cpl. Bankier wounded at the roadside; the remaining defenders of the Shing Mun Redoubt were either trapped in the OP or were starting to withdraw in scattered groups towards the south-east for 5/7 Rajput. Of the pillboxes, 402 was still holding out. As the battle heated up, Maj. Nishiyana brought up his 2nd Company to try and capture this stubborn pillbox. After several attempts, at around 0230hrs in the morning, the Japanese brought up sappers with explosives; Sapper Cpl. Fujimori Sakae and three others forced explosives down the air vent and blew up the pillbox.

Meanwhile rear elements of the 3/228th continued to pour across the dam and advance along the dyke and some pushed down the valley. A group of Rajputs was out patrolling, just as the attack began; as they heard the noise, they were proceeded rapidly towards the redoubt and in the river valley (south-west of the dam) chanced upon some 200 Japanese and immediately engaged the attackers. This firefight continued throughout the attack on the redoubt and the Rajputs even managed to drive the attacking Japanese back up the river valley to the redoubt itself.

Sensing that the redoubt was in trouble, Lt. Col. White moved D Coy 2 Royal Scots from Castle Peak Road to Golden Hill and C Coy, less one platoon, which was to guard the Castle Peak Road junction vacated by D Coy, from Texaco Peninsula (near today's Tusen Wan) to the area of 2 Royal Scots HQ.

10 However, visitors to the Shing Mun Redoubt can see that there are five entrances to the OP, three hatches and an entrance via Strand Palace Hotel, as well as an observation platform, which anyone can climb in and out of with relative ease – it is a mystery why Capt. Jones and his party claimed to have been locked in the OP in subsequent battle reports.

The Japanese were held for some three hours and at last managed to blow up the steel shutters of the OP and in the process killed two Indian signallers; Thompson was badly wounded in the eye by a grenade; Jones and WO2 Mead, the company sergeant-major were both wounded. Stunned, the remaining 15 defenders surrendered and 11 became casualties. With the OP lost, communication to the 2 Royal Scots HQ was also lost. In an attempt to facilitate a counter-attack, the defenders' long-range batteries (notably on the filter beds, Taipo Road, Stonecutters Island and Mt Davis) bombarded the redoubt for two hours till 0500hrs. As the artillery opened up, Capt. Newton of D Coy, 5/7 Rajputs, reported that 19 men had arrived at D Coy's location and, despite the wounded, 13 of them took up position on the left of D Coy. One last pillbox managed to hold out for another 11 hours but it too was blown up; the Japanese dug out four survivors. By 0400hrs on 10 December, the redoubt was entirely lost. For the cost of a mere two killed the Japanese won a strategic victory that tipped the balance of the entire campaign. By the morning a Japanese flag was seen flying proudly on Point 225.

THE LOSS OF KOWLOON

'This was calamitous,' wrote Maltby, 'for Shing Mun was the key to the whole of the left position.' While the British felt the loss of Shing Mun was a disaster, the Japanese saw otherwise. Paradoxically, having punched a hole in the British line, Doi to his astonishment was ordered to withdraw by his superior for he had entered into 230th Regiment's sector and had not followed the carefully prepared war plans. Doi refused to obey the order and, after much argument with Ito and Sakai, his initiative was later censured. A divisional staff officer Oyadomani was made the scapegoat and he was sharply rebuked for not curbing Doi's enthusiasm.

With the redoubt in Japanese hands, Doi was pouring troops into the area and throughout the 10th the Japanese were unsure of their gains and decided on a cautious approach taking advantage of the British disarray to send out small-scale probing patrols. Wallis, the commander of the KIB, ordered the 2 Royal Scots to counter-attack immediately at dawn with support from the Rajputs and artillery, but Lt. Col. White, CO of the Royal Scots, refused, on account of his battalion having no chance of success. As a result the 'counter-attack' on Shing Mun, if it could be called that, was only a half-hearted affair. At first light on 11 December, the Japanese put in a forceful effort on Golden Hill but were stopped by Newton's 5/7 Rajputs and support from 6in. shells from

IJN soldiers of the 230th Regiment rushing to the Star Ferry Pier area in Tsim Sha Tsui. In the background is the clock tower of the then Kowloon Canton Railway Terminus. This clock tower still stands, as does the Star Ferry Pier. (Author's collection)

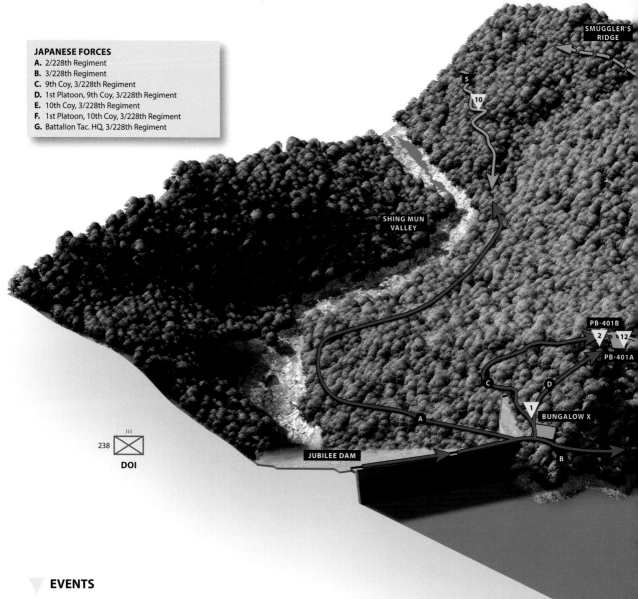

JAPANESE FORCES
A. 2/228th Regiment
B. 3/228th Regiment
C. 9th Coy, 3/228th Regiment
D. 1st Platoon, 9th Coy, 3/228th Regiment
E. 10th Coy, 3/228th Regiment
F. 1st Platoon, 10th Coy, 3/228th Regiment
G. Battalion Tac. HQ, 3/228th Regiment

▼ EVENTS

1. Lt. Kasugai Yoshitaro, commander of 9th Company, 3/228th, crossed the Jubilee Dam past Bungalow X and reached point 255 (PB-401b) by 2130hrs on 9 December 1941, totally undetected.

2. By 2200hrs, 2nd Lt. Yamada Shoji of 1st Platoon, 9th Company, 3/228th, having cut through two layers of barbed wire laid in wait just by PB-401a and PB-401b.

3. Seeing the progress made by 9th Company, Maj. Nishiyana the CO of the 3/228th, ordered Lt. Wakabayashi Touiti and his 10th Coy to take PB-403. Lt. Wakabayashi ordered 1st Platoon, 10th Coy, to lead the attack. On capturing the Shing Mum Redoubt, Lt. Wakabayashi's men carved 'Captured by Wakabayashis unit' in Japanese on the wall just next to the entrance to Shaftesbury Avenue. This is still visible today.

4. At almost the same time, 2300hrs, L/Cpl J. Laird who was on sentry duty in PB-401b heard noises in the bush and opened fire. The Japanese responded with grenades and gunfire and immediately charged the pillboxes.

5. Cpl. Campbell at PB-402 on hearing the gunfire turned his Vickers machine gun and fired towards PB-401a and 401b. Members of the 3/228th HQ were caught in the open and became casualties.

6. Capt. L.C. Wilcox, the FOO of 1st HK Regiment HKSRA, called down FPF fire on the redoubt.

7. Some Indian sentries (from the FOO party) and four members of the Royal Scots on the northern most position abandoned their post and withdraw south to the OP. They entered the OP via the top hatches.

8. 2nd Lt. Mochizuki of 10th Company infiltrated the redoubt and reached the OP. They immediately began to attack the OP and tried to gain entry by the top hatches.

9. The remaining members of the Redoubt not trapped began withdrawing in scattered groups to the location of D Coy, 5/7 Rajputs, location, south-east of the Redoubt.

10. A party of 5/7 Rajputs from D Coy was out patrolling the Shing Mun Valley during the attack. On hearing the commotion they proceeded to the Redoubt and encountered a group of IJA. A fierce firefight broke out and the Rajputs succeeded in driving the IJA back up the valley to the Redoubt.

11. After attacking the OP for nearly three hours the IJA succeeded in blowing up the steel doors of the OP and captured all inside. Two Indian signallers were killed and Lt. J.S.R. Thompson, platoon commander of 8th Platoon was wounded in the eye and temporary blinded. Capt. C. R. Jones the OC of A Coy, 2 Royal Scots, was also wounded. In total 15 were captured.

12. At about 0300hrs, Capt. H. R. Newton OC of D Coy, 5/7 Rajputs, reported some 19 British soldiers arrived at his location, 13 were lightly wounded and took up positions on his left. By 0400hrs on 10 December the Japanese flag proudly flew on Point 255. The Shing Mum Redoubt had been captured.

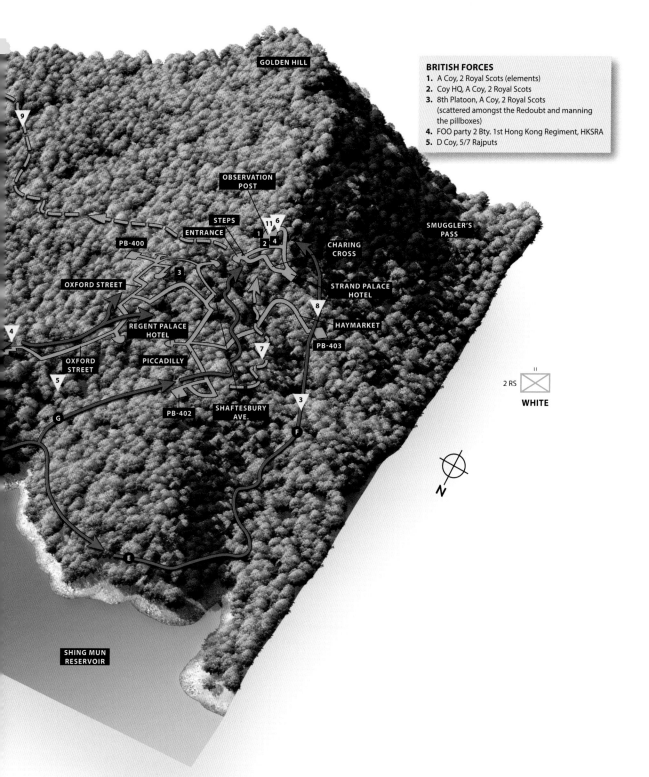

BRITISH FORCES
1. A Coy, 2 Royal Scots (elements)
2. Coy HQ, A Coy, 2 Royal Scots
3. 8th Platoon, A Coy, 2 Royal Scots (scattered amongst the Redoubt and manning the pillboxes)
4. FOO party 2 Bty. 1st Hong Kong Regiment, HKSRA
5. D Coy, 5/7 Rajputs

GOLDEN HILL

OBSERVATION POST

STEPS

ENTRANCE

PB-400

OXFORD STREET

REGENT PALACE HOTEL

OXFORD STREET

PICCADILLY

PB-402

SHAFTESBURY AVE.

SMUGGLER'S PASS

CHARING CROSS

STRAND PALACE HOTEL

HAYMARKET

PB-403

2 RS WHITE

N

SHING MUN RESERVOIR

THE JAPANESE ATTACK ON THE SHING MUN REDOUBT, 9–10 DECEMBER 1941

The Shing Mun Redoubt on the left flank of the Gin Drinkers Line was the Achilles heel of the British defence on the Mainland. The loss of the redoubt saw the collapse of the whole Line and the loss of Kowloon in rapid succession.

The front page of a Japanese wartime propaganda magazine – a Christmas special edition – depicts Mitsubishi Ki-21 (Army Type 97 Heavy Bomber) 'Sally' bombers flying over Hong Kong Island. What would later be known as HMS *Tamar* can clearly be seen towards the bottom on the left-hand side of the magazine. (Author's collection)

HMS *Cicala*[11], which had been covering the left flank of 2 Royal Scots. Lieutenant-Colonel White instead deployed D Coy to take up a position on Golden Hill where there were only shallow shell scrapes and rusted wires, which did nothing to stop the attacking Japanese. Captain D. Pinkerton, the OC of D Coy, 2 Royal Scots, personally led a bayonet charge to clear the Japanese temporarily off the hill on the morning of 11 December, allowing the withdrawal of the wounded and survivors. Some of the casualties were caused by poorly aimed British artillery. B, C and D Coys took the full force of the Japanese attacks with heavy losses to all three companies, so much so that both Capts. W. R. T. Rose and F. S. Richardson, the OCs of B and C Coys, were killed. With the Royal Scots having vacated, X Coy, Winnipeg Grenadiers, and three Bren carriers of No. 1 Coy, HKVDC, and two armoured cars pushed west to cover the gap between Taipo Road and Castle Peak Road, on the left of D Coy, 2 Royal Scots, stretching out in a line running all the way to Shumshuipo. The Rajputs and Punjabis were virtually untouched throughout.

During the attack on Shing Mun, Maltby was distracted by reports of the Japanese landing on Lantau Island, south-west of Hong Kong. The attack was eventually driven off by heavy long-range artillery fire and a second probing attack on Aberdeen (the SNLF was only some 300 yards from the Aberdeen Naval Base but was driven off by machine-gun fire from the Winnipeg Grenadiers and the guns of 3 Bty. HKVDC). In hindsight these were nothing more than diversionary attacks and were never intended to be the main effort of the Japanese. The diversion worked: Maltby kept his garrison reserves, the Middlesex and the two Canadian battalions on Hong Kong Island. If Wallis could have put in a forceful counter-attack on 10 December with the 2 Royal Scots and brigade reserve, the Rajputs could have driven the Japanese off the vital ground of Shing Mun since, for most of the 10th, the Japanese were still in disarray after the unexpected success of then 228th Regiment, and Col. Doi had been brought before an irate Sakai who had flown down specially from Guangzhou to Taipo, New Territories, the HQ of the 38th Division, for a pre-court-martial hearing.

Maltby now decided, after only 48 hours of fighting, that it was too risky to attempt to hold the mainland and the three battalions there were to be brought back intact to Hong Kong Island to take up their allocated role in the defence of fortress Hong Kong. The security of Hong Kong Island was always the first consideration, and there was never any intention to make an all-out stand on the mainland. The naval commodore protested that he was not ready to carry out the necessary demolition, transfer of stores or the ferrying of troops across to the island, and so the order to evacuate the mainland was delayed 24 hours until noon of 11 December.

---

11 HMS *Cicala* was hit on the stern and retired. HMS *Tern* replaced *Cicala* covering the left flank of the Gin Drinkers Line.

At noon the decision was made for the mainland to be evacuated under cover of darkness. Further demolition was carried out, including the China Light & Power (CLP) Station as well as the cement works on Tsing Yi Island. The docks were also destroyed. However even at this late stage, Wallis still believed that Maltby's order was only a precautionary measure as he did not anticipate a total withdrawal for at least a week. The evacuation plan was designed to avoid the city, where the British force might be delayed by street fighting or attacks by fifth columnists. If the withdrawal had taken place in Kowloon, the British would have had to deal with an IJA advance column of 350 men from the 3/230th that had infiltrated Kowloon on the morning of the 12th to cut off the retreating British. The 2 Royal Scots and the Canadians, along with most of the gunners, retired south to Shamshuipo Barracks and the Jordan Road Pier, located at western Kowloon, while the Rajputs and the supporting artillery were to retire east to Ma Lau Tong which protected the fortified Devil's Peak Peninsula. At this stage Maltby's intention was to retain the Devil's Peak Peninsula up to the Ma Lau Tong line permanently because it occupied a commanding position and could be easily supplied from Hong Kong across the narrow Lyemun Strait.

At this point, the withdrawal was more or less going to plan. The Canadians and Royal Scots withdrew under the cover of the Punjabis and embarked at the pre-arranged points on the afternoon and evening of the 11th. The Punjabis had a more difficult task in making a moonlight trek along the steep Kowloon hills, laden with supplies but without the necessary allocation of mules. One group missed a critical junction and split into two; one proceeded towards Devil's Peak as planned but Bn. HQ came down to Kai Tak Airport and had to go through Kowloon City before being evacuated by Star Ferry at Tsim Sha Tsui, almost at gunpoint, fighting up to the final minute as the last man stepped aboard the ferry. On the night of the 12th the CO of the Rajputs, having failed to make contact with his counterpart in the Punjabis, decided to give up the Ma Lau Tong line and retire to the Hai Wan line, closer to Devil's Peak. By 0400hrs on the 12th, the Punjabis and one company of the Rajputs, plus the gunners of the 25th Medium Bty. HKSRA made it across to Hong Kong Island across the Lyemun Straits. The evacuation continued in the morning, surprisingly without much interference from the Japanese. With the additional effort of the Navy the evacuation was complete by the morning of the 13th, albeit without 170 mules because of the desertion of Chinese labourers. The mules were to be sadly missed in the subsequent campaign. The last to leave was Capt. N. Forsythe OC of C Coy, 2/14 Punjab. During this time, the IJN tried its hand at shore bombardment, but, despite being at the extreme range of the guns of the 30th Bty., the defenders, by virtue of their longer range 9.2in guns, were able to inflict considerable damage on the IJN, in particular its cruiser, even at extreme range; and because of this incident, for much of the remaining battle of Hong Kong, the IJN kept an arm's length from the shores of Hong Kong and played a minor role in the subsequent battle. The decision to withdraw and the speed with which it was done appeared to have taken the Japanese by surprise. The most probable explanation was that the Japanese expected to have to take Devil's Peak by full-scale attack with ample bombardment because, just a day earlier, an infantry attack without any artillery preparation had been driven off with heavy losses, and the Japanese probably thought that the British were stronger than they had anticipated. The defence of the mainland lasted only five days.

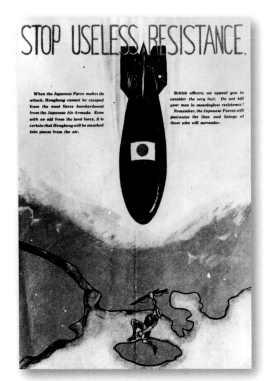

STOP USELESS RESISTANCE.

When the Japanese Forces makes its attack, Hongkong cannot be escaped from the most fierce bombardment from the Japanese Air Armada. Even with no aid from the land force, it is certain that Hongkong will be smashed into pieces from the air.

British officers, we appeal you to consider the very fact. Do not kill your men in meaningless resistance! Remember, the Japanese Forces will guarantee the lives and livings of those who will surrender.

STOP USELESS RESISTANCE – Psychological Operations (PSYOPs) Japanese 1941 style, one of the many propaganda leaflets that the Japanese scattered on Hong Kong Island prior to the invasion of the island. The promise on the leaflets, that the Japanese will 'guarantee' lives for those who surrender, sounds particularly hollow. (Hong Kong Library)

THE LULL BEFORE THE STORM

With the mainland in Japanese hands, the next phase was to launch an assault on Hong Kong Island. The first move was not military but took the form of a peace mission to attempt to persuade Governor Young to surrender. At 0900hrs on 13 December a small boat bearing a white flag crossed the harbour with Col. Toda, Lt. Mizuno[12], Mr Othsu Dak and Mrs Macdonald, a prominent, highly pregnant European and her friend Mrs C. R. Lee, wife of the secretary to the Governor and her two dachshunds. The terms of surrender were categorically rejected. Major Boxer delivered the written rebuff in person. Mrs Macdonald remained in Hong Kong to have her baby, and Mrs Lee, along with her dogs, returned to Kowloon.

The Japanese then began systematically shelling selected targets. On the 13th, a 9.2in. gun on Mt Davis was knocked out and Belcher's Fort was hit. Next day the 3in. gun on Mt Davis was hit, causing casualties among the Chinese gunners; morale collapsed and some deserted. On the 15th the shelling switched to targets on the northern shoreline, deliberately aiming at the pillboxes. At 2100hrs on the same night after some preparatory bombardment, approximately three companies of Japanese attempted to cross the harbour in rubber and improvised rafts towards Pakshawan but were driven off by machine-gun fire. Fifth columnists were also active; some signalled with mirrors, others were used as snipers. One group engaged in propaganda and persuaded the Chinese to desert. Their efforts would have caused more damage if it had not been for Rear-Adm. Chan and Col. Yee with their gangs of 'loyal' Triads. Armed with tommy guns and grenades, they systematically eliminated many of these fifth columnists.

A drawing by Japanese war artist Yuamaguchi Hoshum, depicting Hong Kong under attack. The clock tower on the right is the terminus building of the Kowloon Canton Railway in Tsim Sha Tsui. It still stands and bears war damage from 1941. (Author's collection)

12 A week earlier, Mizuno had been a sports store manager in Hong Kong.

On 13 December 1941 the Japanese delegation on Kowloon Docks is about to depart for Hong Kong Island on a 'peace' mission. The man in the centre is holding a folded white banner, which will be unveiled with the words 'PEACE MISSION' on it. (Author's collection)

This captured Japanese war map depicts the situation just after Kowloon was evacuated on the 13th and invasion of Hong Kong Island on the 18th. This map shows the bombardment zone, landing and embarkation locations, unit boundaries as well as phase lines with dates. What is interesting is that the IJA envisaged that the final assault on Victoria City would commence on 19th; however, the stand at Wongneichong Gap on the 19th total derailed the IJA timetable and it was not until 25th that the defenders surrendered. (Author's collection)

Despite the efforts of the gunners and the Navy, the Japanese continued to round up boats in preparation for the crossing. By the 16th, half of the pillboxes between the racecourse and the Lyemun Straits had been destroyed; it was clear where the crossing would occur. On the morning of the 17th the Japanese sent a second peace mission, this time with the same Japanese team accompanied by two women hostages – Mrs Lee with her two dachshunds and a pregnant Russian woman. Their overtures were again bluntly rejected. On the 18th the bombardment intensified still further, and all indicators pointed to an imminent assault; the oil storage tanks were hit and set on fire, and for some days a pall of dense black smoke covered the north-east corner of the island, giving perfect cover to the Japanese.

THE ASSAULT ON HONG KONG

By the night of the 14th, units evacuated from the mainland had taken up new positions on the island. The defence was now reorganized into the East and West Brigades. Brigadier Wallis commanded the East Brigade with headquarters at Taitam Gap, while Brigadier Lawson acted as CO of West Brigade with headquarters at the Wongneichong Gap. The former included the 5/7 Rajputs holding pillboxes on the north-east perimeter of Hong Kong Island, covering a frontage of over 3,500m.

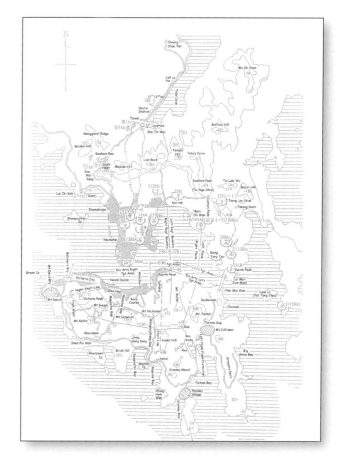

Disposition of artillery on map opposite

8th Costal Regt., 1st Hong Kong Regt. HKSRA – Lt. Col. S. Shaw
(N) 12th Bty –3 x 9.2in. guns – Maj. W. M. Stevenson
(L) 30th Bty – 2 x 9.2in. guns – Maj. C. R. Templer
(K) 36th Bty – 4 x 6in. guns – Maj. W. N. J. Pitt

12th Costal Regt. HKSRA – Lt. Col. R. J. L. Penfold
(A) 24th Bty – 3 x 9.2in. guns – Maj. E. W. S. Anderson
(H) 26th Bty – 3 x 6.in guns – Maj. A. O. G. Mills

965th Defence Bty HKSRA (of 16th Regt. RA but attached to 12th Regt. HKSRA) – Maj. B. T. C. Forrester
(C) No. 1 Troop – 8 x 18-pdrs
(B) No. 2 AA Troop – 2 x 4.7in. QF guns
(G) No. 3 AT Troop – 6 x 2-pdr AT guns

(M) 5th AA Regt HKSRA – Lt. Col. F. D. Field
7th AA Bty – 8 x 3.7in. AA and 3in. guns – Maj. W. A. C. H. Morgan
18th AA Bty – 8 x 40mm Bofors and 6 x Lewis Guns – Maj. J.C. Rochfort-Boyd

17th AA Bty – 8 x 3.7in. and 3in. guns – Maj. A. R. Colquhoun
(J) 1st and (E) 2nd Mountain Bty HKSRA
Each has two troops with one troop equipped with 2x 3.7in howitzers and second troop with 2 x 4.5in. howitzer
(I) No. 3, (D) No. 4 and (F) No. 25 Medium Bty HKSRA
Each battery has 2 x 6in. howitzers
(i) 1st (Coastal Artillery) Bty HKVDC – 2 x 4in. naval guns – Capt. G. F. Rees
(ii) 2nd (Coastal Artillery) Bty HKVDC – 2 x 6in. naval guns – Capt. D. J. S. Crozier
(iii) 3rd (Coastal Artillery) Bty HKVDC – 2 x 4in. naval guns – Capt. C. W. L. Cole
(iv) 4th (Coastal Artillery) Bty HKVDC – 2 x 6in. guns – Capt. K. M. A. Barnett
(v) 5th AA Bty HKVDC – 3in. guns – Capt. L. Goldman

In depth, B Coy was located on the hills behind Taikoo Docks[13], co-located with battalion HQ and a reserve company at Taihang village just north of Causeway Bay. The Royal Rifles of Canada's battalion HQ were at Taitam Gap, covering the north-east corner of Hong Kong, from the west at Stanley to the south with a reserve company at Lyemun. There were two companies of the HKVDC – No. 1 Coy at Taitam Valley and No. 2 Coy at Pottinger Gap (today's Ma Tong Au, an area of low ground north-east of Mt Collinson, south-west of Pottinger Peak). The old soldiers of the Hughsiliers defended the North Point power station. In support were British coastal and field artillery as well as Nos. 1, 2, 4 and 5th Btys. of the HKVDC, the latter being an anti-aircraft unit.

The West Brigade comprised 2/14 Punjab, with their tactical area of responsibility stretching off the northern-west shore of Hong Kong Island from Causeway Bay to Belcher's Point, also defending the Governor's House and Maltby's HQ. The Punjabis' HQ was located on MacDonnell Road, at Mid-Level. The Winnipeg Grenadiers had their battalion HQ at Wanchai Gap, in a defence role, covering the south-west corner of Hong Kong Island with one company detached to defend the brigade HQ at Wongneichong Gap. The Middlesex Regiment was spread out along 72 pillboxes dotted around the entire shoreline of the island. One improvised company, Z Coy, comprising 'odds and sods' – cooks, musicians etc. – was located at Leighton Hill, just north of Causeway Bay, defending the battalion HQ. The 2 Royal Scots, having being badly mauled, were now reinforced with replacements from the HKVDC and held in reserve at Wanchai Gap. The HKVDC's

Men of No. 2 (Scottish) Coy, HKVDC, parading in Wanchai on the last Sunday before the start of the Pacific War. The OC, Major Henry Russell Forsyth, was killed in a desperate rearguard action on the night of 23 December 1941. For his actions Forsyth was awarded a mention in dispatches. (Hong Kong Library)

13 Now part of Taikoo Estate.

Hong Kong Island, the morning of 18 December 1941

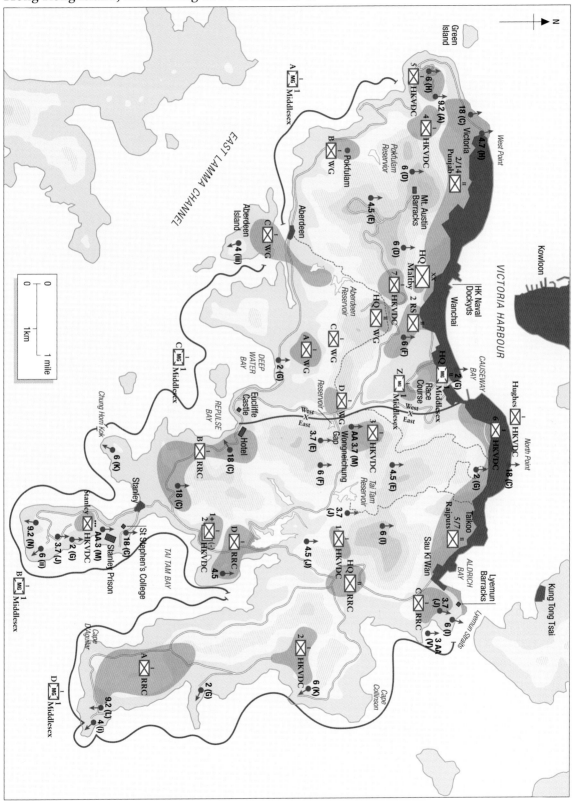

51

IJA troops landing on Hong Kong Island. These troops were all carrying Type 38 rifles, the standard rifle of the Japanese throughout World War II. The long bayonets would have been blackened for night operations. Note that the landing craft are merely boats and not dedicated landing craft. (Author's collection)

No. 4 Coy was at High West, No. 5 Coy at Mt Davis, No. 6 Coy in an anti-aircraft role was deployed along the northern shores of Hong Kong Island. No. 7 Coy was at Magazine Gap high on the hills of Hong Kong and No. 3 Coy at Jardine's Lookout. The HKVDC's HQ was at Peak Mansion on the Peak. Artillery in support of the brigade consisted of 9.2in. and 6in. guns on Mt Davis, and 4.7in. guns at Belcher's Point. No. 3 Bty. HKVDC was located in Aberdeen to protect the naval base.

On the night of the 17th, the Japanese sent out two reconnaissance teams. One failed, but the one team from the 3/229th, led by Lt. Masushima Zempei, managed to swim ashore at Taikoo. Despite being detected and shot at they managed to escape unhurt. An additional 18 bombers from the 14th Heavy Bomber Regiment from Guangzhou and another 18 Navy bombers and 26 fighters from Taizhong (Taichung), Taiwan, were brought over to assist. The crescendo of shelling on the 18th, with dive-bombing and the amassing of small craft on the Kowloon side all pointed to a Japanese assault that night. In preparation for the crossing the Japanese moved all the headquarters forward. The 23rd Army moved its HQ to Taipo in the New Territories, while the divisional HQ of the 38th Division was shifted to Ma Tau Wei, just off Tai-Tak Airport. The deposition of the Hong Kong Island invasion force was as follows:

	Infantry	Artillery	Engineers/bridging materials
Right flank units	Div Inf. Group HQ 2/228th: 1st wave 1/228th plus HQ/228: 2nd wave 3/228th: held back* 3/230th: 1st wave 2/230th plus HQ/230: 2nd wave 1/230th: held back*	5th Ind. Rapid-fire Gun Bn. 1st Bty. 38th Mt. Arty Regt.	38th Eng. Regt. Less 1 Coy
Left flank units	3/229th: 1st wave 2/229th plus HQ/229th: 2nd wave	2nd Ind. Rapid-fire Gun Bn. less 1 Coy 5th Coy of 10th Ind. Mt. Arty Regt.	1 Coy 38th Eng. Regt.
Right artillery		38th Mt. Arty. Regt. less 1st Bn.	
Left artillery	1 Plt. 229th	10th Ind. Mt. Arty. less 1 Coy 20th Ind. Mt. Arty. Regt. 21st Mor. Bn. 1 Coy 2nd Ind. Rapid-fire Gun Bn.	
Landing engineers			20th Ind. Eng. Regt. 1st and 2nd River Crossing Material Coy of 9th Div. with 18 motorized boats and over 200 collapsible rafts
Landing support	5th Coy of 10th Ind. Mt. Arty Regt.	1 Coy 38th Eng. Regt.	2nd Coy 14th Ind. Eng. Regt.
Divisional reserve	1/229th (less 1 Plt.)		

The attacks by MTBs 7 and 9, 19 December 1941

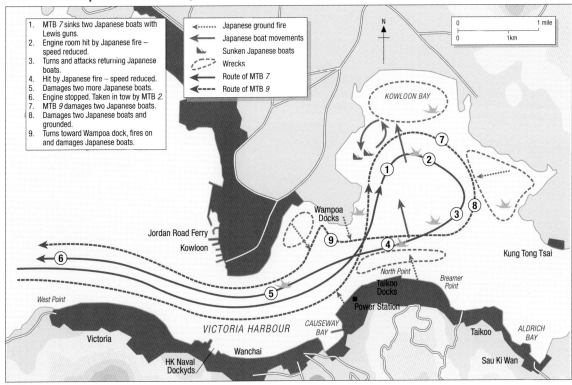

The right flank was to embark east and west of Kai Tak Airport, while the left flank would step off from the Devil's Hill area. The order for invasion was issued at Shatin at 1800hrs; by 1930hrs Sakai and Higuchi, the deputy Chief of Staff, had arrived at Kowloon to supervise the crossing personally. At 2000hrs, H-Hour, 2/228th Regiment silently embarked in small collapsible craft and began paddling with towards their objectives of the Taikoo Docks and nearby sugar factory; the artillery support also commenced. Colonel Doi climbed onto a large barge with 80 members of his TAC HQ and crossed the harbour with 1/228th as part of the second wave. The weather was perfect; it was a moonless night and showery; thick black smoke from burning oil tanks aided the crossing and the Japanese were able to get half way without detection. Then, searchlights and machine-gun fire forced the boats to scatter; as a result commanders were separated from their units. Both 2/228th and 3/230th battalion commanders were wounded and Doi was forced to take over the direct assault. At 2140hrs precisely the artillery switched to depth targets and just five minutes later the first wave of 3/230th landed at North Point, followed by 2/228th at 2150hrs and 2/229th at 2158hrs. The 2/229th landed at Saiwan and the 3/229th battalion at Aldrich Bay, just west of Lyemun. Three red flares were deployed to signal a successful landing. The Rajputs bore the brunt of the weight of the Japanese onslaught. The 3/320th and 2/228th were directed at positions held by D and C Coys of the 5/7 Rajputs, while 3/229th's landing fell on A Coy. Despite many days of shelling, the Rajputs put up a stiff fight and Japanese losses were heavy. The anti-tank company lost so many men that only one gun could be manned. By midnight, all six battalions had landed but men were forced to wait at the water's edge for some time; wire fencing blocked the

HONG KONG – BATTLE MAP –
1st Bn. 8th–25th DEC 41

A hand-drawn map made by a member of 1 Middlesex whilst in a POW camp, detailing the location of the regiment during the battle of Hong Kong, as well as key events of the battle on the island. (NAM)

way, further delaying the advance, and marauding Bren carriers contributed to the chaos. One hour later Sano arrived at Taikoo. The Japanese plan was to bypass isolated resistance for mopping up later and to press forward to high ground. Overwhelmed by a vastly superior force, the Rajputs lost most of their officers and resistance crumbled.

Despite all indications, Maltby still believed that the main force would come directly at Victoria from Kowloon, therefore he held back on the counter-attack, instead ordering a platoon of the Middlesex along with some Royal Marines and naval personnel, together with the Rajputs' reserve company at Taihang, supported by artillery, to establish a defensive line to block the Japanese advance to Central District. Three armoured cars of the HKVDC were dispatched to protect East Brigade's HQ and two cars went to reinforce the Middlesex's battalion HQ, all quite inadequate against six battalions of IJA. In the post-war dispatches, Maltby admitted that he totally underestimated the Japanese landing. He thought that he was facing at most two battalions.

THE BATTLE OF NORTH POINT POWER STATION

As the 3/230th broke through D Coy, 5/7 Rajputs, the 2/230th also came ashore in the vicinity and turned westwards towards Victoria City, but the advance was blocked by a group of older men of the HKVDC's Hughsiliers Platoon holed up in the North Point power station. There were four officers and 36 men of the HKVDC, 39 volunteers of the CLP and HK Electric, including Pte. Vincent Sorby, the manager of the power station, as well as eight Free French and their commander, Capt. Jacques Egal (a former representative of the Free French in Shanghai, and a wealthy wine trader who happened to be in Hong Kong on 8 December). All were old World War I veterans and some had even fought in the Boer War; without exception all were over the age of 55 and they managed to hold up the entire Japanese 230th Regiment. Major, the Honourable J. J. Patterson, OC Hughsiliers, had once served with Allenby's Camel Corps and had been mentioned in dispatches six times. He was at the time the Chairman of Jardine Matterson, a prodigious trading house (which still exists today) and a member of the legislative council; Pte. Sir Edward Des Voeux 8th Baronet, nephew of a former Hong Kong Governor, millionaire gold bullion trader and secretary of the prestigious Hong Kong Club, enlisted as a private after he was found to be too old for mobilization duties. Private T. A. Pearce, 67 years young, Chairman of J. D. Hutchison & Co., secretary of the Hong Kong Jockey Club; Capt. Bruch, second in command, was 60 and chairman of trading

Japanese Type 94 tankettes on the march in Causeway Bay, Hong Kong, with the North Point power station in the background. The Type 94 was a 3-ton two-man thinly armoured tankette, which could be penetrated by 0.30in. armour-piercing rounds at ranges up to 300m. (Hong Kong Library)

house Moutire & Co.; the list goes on. Under pressure, Patterson called for help and Maltby dispatched an HKVDC armoured car with a platoon from Z Coy, 1 Middlesex, but it was ambushed before reaching the power station. Only nine managed to reach it, including 2nd Lt. Caruthers, the armoured car commander. Unable to dislodge the old men, the IJA decided to bombard the power station into submission. Captain Frédéric Jacosta, Head of Free French Military Intelligence in Singapore, was in Hong Kong visiting his friend Egal when the war started and both decided to join the HKVDC. Jacosta advised Sir Edward to withdraw to a safer place. Sir Edward said 'he was far too old go dashing about and preferred to fight in comfort.' Shortly after, Sir Edward was killed by mortar splinters. He was 77 years old.

At 0145hrs on the 19th, the Hughsiliers reported the power station surrounded. Outnumbered by twenty to one and with ammunition exhausted, Pte. Pearce, Geoghan, V. Sorby, J. Roscoe and Cpl. R. P. Dunlop of the Middlesex withdrew to King's/Electric Road and continued to fight using a broken-down bus as cover. Sorby was shot in both knees. The Japanese tried to rush the bus but were defeated; Dunlop and Roscoe were mortally injured from sword wounds. The Japanese deployed three machine guns, killing or

IJA troops advancing on Hong Kong Island, probably 18–19 December 1941. Below is North Point and in the background is the Kowloon Peninsula, looking north-west. Note the sunken ships in the harbour; many had been scuttled to deny them to the IJA. This picture was likely to have been taken on Braemer Hill or the lower slopes of Mt Butler. (Author's collection)

An IJA Type 41 75mm mountain gun in the area of the North Point power station. The Type 41 could be split into seven parts, each carried by a horse. Each gun was served by a crew of one NCO and nine men and backed up by a section of ammunition bearers, usually made up of two horses, one NCO and 12 men. (Author's collection)

seriously wounding all except Geoghan. Expecting that all were killed, a Japanese officer carefully approached the bus, but Geoghan despite being wounded, was still in fighting mood. He leapt up and charged the Japanese officer, killing him and four soldiers. Somehow Geoghan survived. The old men halted the westward advance of the entire Japanese IJA for 18 hours, enabling Maltby to withdraw forces and to establish a new front line.

THE ANNIHILATION OF EAST BRIGADE

While the 2/229th Regt. moved south uphill towards Mt Parker, the 3/229th landed at Aldrich Bay, turned eastwards towards Lyemun and captured an HKVDC 6in. gun. Unaware of the landing, Maj. Bishop, OC C Coy, Royal Rifles of Canada, dispatched 15 Platoon under Lt. Scott to check on A Coy, Rajputs, when unexpectedly 15 Platoon exchanged fire with a group of armed men in civilian clothes at the gate of Lyemun garrison. At first, as with so many other early reports, accounts of Japanese landings and loss of position were not taken seriously by senior officers, so much so that, at the garrison at Lyemun Fort, 5th Anti-aircraft Bty. HKVDC was taken completely by surprise and was captured after only a brief fight. The Japanese then started to commit one of many massacres by bayoneting 29 survivors. Alerted by 15 Platoon's report, Bishop decided to conduct a counter-attack to retake the fort with 13 and 15 Platoons, but failed to scale a 6m wall and retired with nine men killed.

As the 2/229th proceeded southwards uphill to Mt Parker they came upon the Salesian Mission which was now acting as an Advance Dressing Station. No. 8 Coy 2/229th entered the Mission and were instructed to kill all of the medical personnel and injured. In the confusion, Gunners Y. K. Chan, Martin H. C. Tso of the 5th Bty., Capt. Osler Thomas HKVDC, Capt. Martin Banfill RCMC and Cpl. Norman Leath RAMC from the Mission survived the ordeal and lived to testify at the war crimes trial of Col. Tanaka. Reinforced with extra machine guns, some left behind by fleeing Rajputs, C Coy gave the Japanese a bloody nose and caused one Japanese company to suffer over 65 per cent casualties. Unable to get past the Canadians,

The invasion of Hong Kong Island, 18–25 December 1941

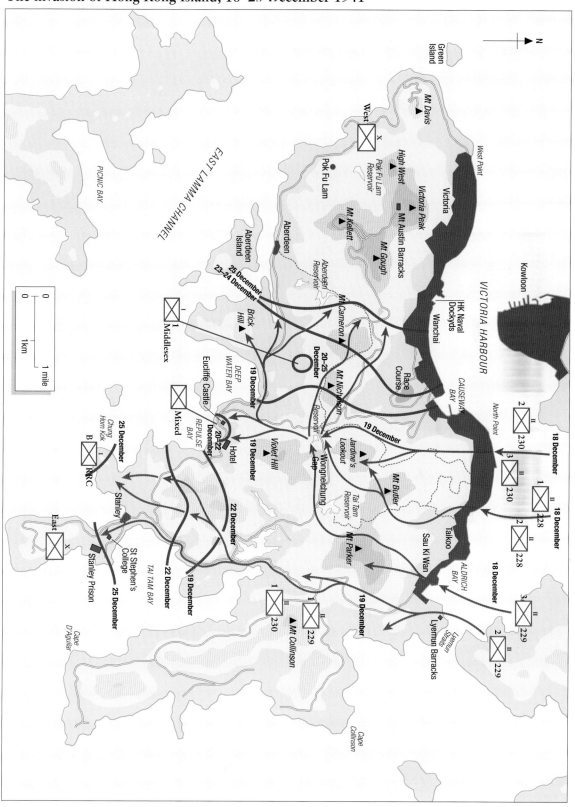

ASHBY LEADS THE ATTACK AT VICTORIA HARBOUR – CHARGE OF THE NAVAL LIGHT BRIGADE (PP. 58–59)

At 0845hrs on the morning of 19 December 1941, six MTBs (British power boats – 60ft class), Nos. 7, 9, 11, 12, 27 and 26, are massing off the north-western coast of Hong Kong Island beyond Green Island, under the command of Lt. R. R. W. Ashby HKRNVR. Ashby decides to attack in pairs and he is leading with the first pair. This first pair, MTBs 7 and 9, head off into Victoria Harbour travelling from west to east; 7 is the more northerly of the MTBs as they travel across the harbour, passing the ferry pier on the southern edge of Kowloon Peninsula, and then past the Kowloon Canton Rail (KCR) terminus, to the east of the ferry pier, to Holt's Wharf. When just outside Holt's Wharf, around 200m ahead to the north-north-east, they see a cluster of Japanese craft including a motor boat towing some wooden sampans (1). This group of three craft, with about 15–20-odd Japanese on each of the boats attempting to cross the harbour, is leading the cluster. At the command of Ashby, MTB 7 immediately pushes to full speed at 37

knots towards the Japanese with all its Lewis guns (a pair each at the front and the rear, plus a spare at the bridge) blazing (2). As MTB 7 moves in to attack, a flight of Japanese Ki-27 (Nate) fighters, on station above the harbour, provides air cover and immediately dives to shower the two MTBs with machine-gun fire (3). At the same time Japanese troops on their craft begin to return fire, disturbing the water around the MTB. At 100m 7 begins firing and 9 joins in, although, for the most part, the latter's line of fire is blocked by the former. MTB 7 comes as close as 5m (point blank) to the leading Japanese craft, with all guns on full auto. It also drops two depth charges but they fail to explode because of the shallowness of the water, being so close to the wharf. Nevertheless all boats burst into flames and capsize on account of the wake generated by MTB 7. Lieutenant Ashby reported no survivors. He was awarded the DSC for this action.

the Japanese moved around the flank of the Royal Rifles of Canada. The encounter also left the Canadians with heavy casualties, losing almost two platoons. In need of replenishment C Coy withdrew leaving only one reinforcement platoon from A Coy under Lt. Blaver on Mt Parker. At about 0300hrs Capt. Clerke from HQ Coy was ordered to take 16 Platoon from D Coy, Royal Rifles of Canada, to reinforce Mt Parker, but poor navigation caused the Canadians to lose their way and they did not arrive at their destination until 0730hrs. Clerke found that over 100 Japanese had already occupied Mt Parker, with Blaver fighting a desperate rearguard action. With only two platoons and no artillery support, Clerke could never hope to defeat over 100 Japanese and decided to withdraw, leaving Mt Parker in Japanese hands.

At the end of the day, it had been a disaster for the East Brigade. The infantry force was halved, and even more embarrassing were the losses to the artillery. A series of mix-ups and misinterpretations of orders caused the coastal guns at Capes D'Aguilar and Collinson to be destroyed and abandoned, either accidently or deliberately. In the confusion, one troop of 965 Bty. destroyed its guns in error while another lost its guns to the Japanese. What was left were one 18-pdr and two 3.7in. field guns.

18 December 1941 edition of *Asahi Shimbun*, a top-selling Japanese newspaper of the day, showing a report on the battle of Hong Kong on the front page. The picture at the top left shows the sinking of HMS *Prince of Wales* and *Repulse*. (Author's collection)

THE BATTLE OF THE WONGNEICHONG GAP

Wongneichong, or yellow muddy creek in Chinese, is located in the centre of Hong Kong Island, separating Mt Parker (532m), Mt Butler (436m) and Jardine's Lookout (433m) to the east from Mt Nicholson (430m), Mt Cameron (410m), Mt Gough (384m) and Victoria Peak (552m) to the west. This valley forms a vital communication route linking the north of Hong Kong to the south. Brigadier Lawson placed the West Brigade HQ on this vital ground. Realizing its exposed position after the landing on the 18th, Maj. Lyndon, the brigade major, located a new site for the Brigade HQ to the south of Mt Nicholson and scheduled the move for the following day.

In response to the landing, Lawson dispatched three platoons from the Winnipeg Grenadiers to block the Japanese advance. Lt. C. D. French took 18 Platoon to Mt Butler, Lt. G. A. Birkett's 17 Platoon went to Jardine's Lookout and Lt. L. B. Corrigan's platoon moved to the north-west of the Gap. As on Mt Parker, Birkett's and French's platoons had as much success as one might expect after being sent to meet battalions-worth of enemy with artillery support. Both Birkett and French were killed and survivors went on to HKVDC's pillboxes, holding out until the afternoon. By the morning of the 19th two battalions of 230th and two battalions of the 228th were pushing for the hills. The 2/230th moved rapidly to occupy Jardine's Lookout, while the 3/230th moved to occupy Mt Nicholson and the 2/228th headed towards the Gap. No. 3 Coy, HKVDC, under Maj. E. Stewart occupied pillboxes around Jardine's Lookout, while No. 1 Coy, HKVDC, under Capt. Penn was holding positions around Taitam Valley with forward positions in Quarry Gap, south-west of Jardine's Lookout. The pillboxes were soon overwhelmed but not before the Japanese suffered heavy casualties. Some managed to hold out for 24 hours. Stewart held his Coy HQ until the 22nd, ensuring four days of continuous fighting until exhausted by lack of ammunition, food and water. In the battle of Wongneichong, No. 3 Coy, HKVDC, suffered 80 per cent casualties and ceased to exist as a formation.

Lawson realized that the enemy had penetrated as far as Mt Butler, and that he needed to counter-attack quickly. D Coy, Winnipeg Grenadiers, was the Brigade Reserve and was holding vital positions in the Gap. Not wishing to expose the position, the only option was to bring up A Coy, Winnipeg Grenadiers, (plus one platoon from D Coy to make up for the platoon that had been left behind), commanded by Maj. A. B. Gresham, to clear the Japanese off Jardine's Lookout and occupy Mt Butler. Gresham did not reach the start line until dawn. Initially the Canadians

IJA troops advancing along Black Links on Hong Kong Island. The long poles carried by these men as seen in the picture were Bangalore torpedoes, pipes filled with explosive used for clearing obstacles such as wires and mines when assaulting the pillboxes. (Author's collection)

were successful in retaking Mt Butler, with WO2 J. R. Osborne leading a bayonet charge. By 2200hrs a strong counter-attack by three companies of Japanese pushed A Coy back, but the Canadians stood firm until about 1500hrs. Major Gresham decided to surrender after exhausting all the ammunition, but he was shot despite holding a white flag. In the confusion a Canadian shot back and killed a Japanese officer and the Japanese responded with a shower of grenades. Warrant Officer 2 Osborne returned the grenades as fast as the Japanese threw them; one landed in an awkward location and could not be picked up; Osborne threw himself on the grenade to save the others. This act of self-sacrifice won him a VC, the first Canadian VC of World War II.

At dawn on the 19th, realizing the desperate situation at the Gap, Maltby dispatched A Coy, 2 Royal Scots, to the rescue under Capt. K. J. Campbell, but they lost all their officers and only 15 men managed to reach the HQ. A group of sailors under Cdr. A. L. Pears came from the south to its aid but, before reaching the Gap, were ambushed and only a few managed to reach a house – the Postbridge – just south of the Gap. Eventually the 3/230th captured the police station located on a mound at the southern point of the Gap; it then moved east and captured the anti-aircraft guns of 7th Bty. (less than 250m from the brigade HQ) and continued uphill towards Taitam Hill (now Parkview Road) to capture more guns – 6in. and 3.7in. In desperation Maltby called down final protective fire from the HKSRA in Happy Valley and inflicted massive casualties on the 3/230th. At about 1000hrs on the 19th, Lawson reported that his HQ was surrounded and he was about to 'go outside and shoot it out'. Captain H. A. Bush was to provide covering fire and Lawson and his entire staff, including the Middlesex signallers, was cut down by machine-gun fire across the Gap. Lawson's body was found two days later by the Japanese, halfway up the hill behind his HQ. He died of loss of blood from a gunshot wound to his thigh. Lieutenant Kerfoot, 2/14 Punjab, with his three Bren carriers arrived a few minutes too late to save Lawson.

At 1330hrs Maltby issued 'Operation Order No. 6' calling for a massive counter-attack to commence some 90 minutes later. The plan was for A and D Coys from the 2/14 Punjab to attack east from Victoria to North Point to relieve the Hughsiliers, but the orders never reached Lt. Col. Kidd, the CO of the Punjabis. HQ Coy Winnipeg Grenadiers on the right (on the north side of Mt Nicholson) and 2 Royal Scots on the left (or the south side) of the Punjabis formed the centre of the line and were to attack the Gap and Jardine's Lookout. Eight field guns were promised but again did not materialize. There was no recce or proper orders given. The plan was for the Canadians to meet up with the 2 Royal Scots at Middle Gap at 1530hrs, but the Scots were late and the Canadians moved ahead without them. The officer commanding D Coy, 2 Royal Scots, was Capt. Pinkerton (attached to the Royal Scots were Capt. K. S. Robertson and Lt. I. P. Tamworth HKVDC,

The St John Ambulance Brigade memorial at the Wongneichong Gap. Located just below the police station, this obelisk records the members of the brigade that were massacred at the Wongneichong Gap. This picture was taken on the Remembrance Sunday parade in 2010. (Author's collection)

COUNTER-ATTACK AT THE WONGNEICHONG GAP (PP. 64–65)

At 1500hrs on 19 December another counter-attack force begins to move on to Wongneichong Gap, but this time it is late setting off as, according to plan, it be at Middle Gap by 1530hrs. By the time it reaches the Gap it is twilight. This counter-attack force is composed of elements of D Coy, 2 Royal Scots, and D Coy, Winnipeg Grenadiers, with Capt. Robertson and Capt. Tamworth of the HKVDC and a group of Chinese sappers acting as infantry. The HKVDC and Chinese sappers are placed under the command of Capt. David Pinkerton, the OC D Coy, 2 Royal Scots, who is also the overall commander of this ad hoc counter-attack force. Leading the advance is Capt. A. M. S. Slater-Brown in a Bren carrier with 2nd Lt. McCallum Bell, the Intelligence Officer of 2 Royal Scots in the second Bren carrier. A third Bren carrier follows on and this forms the vanguard of the attacking force. Moving with the three Bren carriers are Canadian infantrymen from the D Coy, Winnipeg Grenadiers, and Chinese sappers, who accompany the three carriers on foot. The Royal Engineers were one of the few

British Army units in Hong Kong that recruited local Chinese as regular soldiers; many are armed with US-made Thompson sub-machine guns that carry a drum magazine of 50 rounds with potent hitting power. Despite being few in numbers these Hong Kong Chinese soldiers were well regarded as a professional fighting force and were especially mentioned for their contribution by Maltby in his post-war report. This plate depicts the scene moments before the Japanese open fire, as the Bren carriers and infantry **(1)** are just passing the wreckage and the dead from A Coy, 2 Royal Scots **(2)**, who had attacked up the same road just seven hours before. The lack of military transport forced the British to commandeer civilian cars **(3)** throughout the campaign and it was a common sight to see the standard British Army transport of its days, the Morris C8 15-CWT truck, abandoned alongside Bren carriers and civilian cars in the battle of Hong Kong.

commanding a group of sappers acting as infantry) whose task was to move up the south side of Mt Nicholson, via Black's Link, a narrow mountain pass, and attack the south-west side of Jardine's Lookout with a composite company from HQ and B Coy under Capt. D. Ford to his right. C Coy, 2 Royal Scots, was to follow D Coy, Winnipeg Grenadiers. For some unexpected reason the order was changed at the last minute and Pinkerton was told to attack up Wongneichong Gap Road along the same route taken by A Coy, 2 Royal Scots, just seven hours earlier, because it was 'lightly held'. Captain A. M. S. Slater-Brown led the advance with the three remaining Bren carriers and the attached engineers, followed by D Coy, Winnipeg Grenadiers, on foot. Just as the Bren carriers reached the burnt-out trucks of A Coy, they too were ambushed. Mortars and machine-gun fire rained down from Jardine's Lookout, with the Japanese using captured pillboxes from the HKVDC. Captain Slater-Brown and 2nd Lt. Bell, the battalion's intelligence officer, were killed instantly. Crouched beside the ditch by the road, the Royal Scots waited till 0200hrs before launching an attack on the police station, succeeding in reaching the steps before Pinkerton was seriously wounded. The attack by Capt. Ford's composite company at 0300hrs also failed. Almost at the same time an independent action by C Coy, 2 Royal Scots, under Lt. F. L. Stanier attacked Jardine's Lookout and also failed. This series of escapades cost the Royal Scots eight officers and 68 soldiers.

QF 3.7in. anti-aircraft guns of 7th Bty. 5th Heavy Anti-aircraft Regt., shortly after capture by the IJA at the Wongneichong Gap. Note how bare the hills are leading towards Jardine's Lookout in the background; today it is a heavily wooded area. (Author's collection)

Maltby was getting increasingly desperate. He ordered Maj. Hodkinson OC HQ Coy, Winnipeg Grenadiers, to attack the Gap and proceed to Mt Parker. HQ Coy was understrength and Hodkinson asked for a platoon from A Coy, Winnipeg Grenadiers, and reinforcements from the 2 Royal Scots. Covering fire was provided by Lt. Corrigan from Mt Nicholson but the Grenadiers managed to reach Mt Nicholson with five unwounded men, but Corrigan eventually succeeded in advancing just 300m short of the Gap road. While Hodkinson's group was skirting round Black's Link, he suddenly came upon 500 Japanese, probably from

East Brigade HQ at the Wongneichong Gap as it appears today. Lawson tried to run up to the hill behind along the path just to the left of the steps, but was cut down halfway up and died from uncontrolled bleeding. (Author's collection)

JAPANESE FORCES
A. 2/230th Regiment
B. 3/230th Regiment
C. 3/229th Regiment
D. 1/228th Regiment
E. 2/228th Regiment

WEST

LAWSON

MOUNT NICHOLSON

WONGNEICHONG GAP ROAD

BLACK'S LINK

SIR CECIL'S RIDE

DEEPWATER BAY ROAD

WATER CATCHMENT

POLICE STATION

JARDINE'S LOOKOUT

POSTBRIDGE HOUSE

REPULSE BAY ROAD

WONGNEICHONG RESERVOIR

TAITAM ROAD

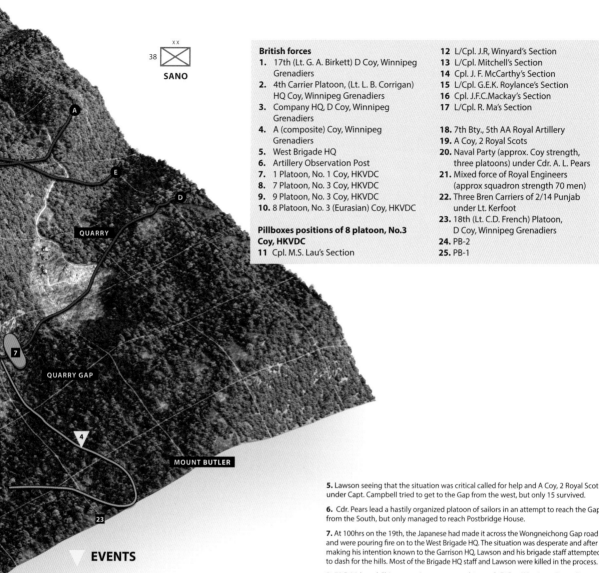

British forces
1. 17th (Lt. G. A. Birkett) D Coy, Winnipeg Grenadiers
2. 4th Carrier Platoon, (Lt. L. B. Corrigan) HQ Coy, Winnipeg Grenadiers
3. Company HQ, D Coy, Winnipeg Grenadiers
4. A (composite) Coy, Winnipeg Grenadiers
5. West Brigade HQ
6. Artillery Observation Post
7. 1 Platoon, No. 1 Coy, HKVDC
8. 7 Platoon, No. 3 Coy, HKVDC
9. 9 Platoon, No. 3 Coy, HKVDC
10. 8 Platoon, No. 3 (Eurasian) Coy, HKVDC

Pillboxes positions of 8 platoon, No.3 Coy, HKVDC
11 Cpl. M.S. Lau's Section

12 L/Cpl. J.R, Winyard's Section
13 L/Cpl. Mitchell's Section
14 Cpl. J. F. McCarthy's Section
15 L/Cpl. G.E.K. Roylance's Section
16 Cpl. J.F.C.Mackay's Section
17 L/Cpl. R. Ma's Section
18. 7th Bty., 5th AA Royal Artillery
19. A Coy, 2 Royal Scots
20. Naval Party (approx. Coy strength, three platoons) under Cdr. A. L. Pears
21. Mixed force of Royal Engineers (approx squadron strength 70 men)
22. Three Bren Carriers of 2/14 Punjab under Lt. Kerfoot
23. 18th (Lt. C.D. French) Platoon, D Coy, Winnipeg Grenadiers
24. PB-2
25. PB-1

EVENTS

1. Shortly after midnight on 19 December Brig. Lawson ordered three blocking columns each of platoon strength to reinforce likely approaches to the Wongneichong Gap. 17th Platoon under Lt. G. A. Birkett of the Winnipeg Grenadiers was on Jardine's Lookout. Lt. French's platoon moved to Mount Butler, east of Jardine's Lookout and Lt. L. B. Corrigan's platoon took up position east of the 7th Bty AA gun position. Around 0500hrs on 19th December, the 2/230th Regiment moved rapidly to occupy Jardine's Lookout, first dealing with 17th Platoon. Birkett tried to clear the Japanese from the hills but was killed in the battle with the survivors moving back towards the Wongneichong Gap. The 2/228th Regiment followed the 2/230th.

2. The 1/228th Regiment came through Quarry Gap, an area of low ground separating Jardine's Lookout and Mount Butler, where they annihilated No. 1 Platoon of Capt. Penn's No. 1 Coy, HKVDC, and proceeded westward towards the Wongneichong Gap Road.

3. Around 0700hrs the 3/320th Regiment came up along the Wongneichong Gap road and Sir Cecil's Ride to reach the position of D Coy, Winnipeg Grenadiers, and the West Brigade HQ. An hour later the 2/230th Regiment also came through and proceeded to take up positions east of the Wongneichong Gap Road facing the West Brigade HQ.

4. As the Japanese were approaching Jardine's Lookout, Lawson dispatched A Coy, Winnipeg Grenadiers, under Maj. A. B. Gresham. As the Japanese had already taken Jardine's Lookout and Mount Butler, Gresham was now ordered to clear both locations of Japanese forces. In the ensuing battle, A Coy was initially successful in reaching Mount Butler, but was driven back with Maj. Gresham was killed in the process.

5. Lawson seeing that the situation was critical called for help and A Coy, 2 Royal Scots under Capt. Campbell tried to get to the Gap from the west, but only 15 survived.

6. Cdr. Pears lead a hastily organized platoon of sailors in an attempt to reach the Gap from the South, but only managed to reach Postbridge House.

7. At 100hrs on the 19th, the Japanese had made it across the Wongneichong Gap road and were pouring fire on to the West Brigade HQ. The situation was desperate and after making his intention known to the Garrison HQ, Lawson and his brigade staff attempted to dash for the hills. Most of the Brigade HQ staff and Lawson were killed in the process.

8. 70 British and Chinese engineers managed to reach D Coy, Winnipeg Grenadiers. The Canadians were the last to surrender, holding out until the 22nd.

9. The 3/230th Regiment proceeded to clear the positions along the Wongneichong Gap. They met with stiff resistance at the police station that required the use of QF guns; the defenders in Postbridge House continue to hold out.

10. By midday the only positions in the Gap area still holding out were elements of No. 3 Coy, HKVDC, elements of D Coy, Winnipeg Grenadiers, and pillboxes PB-1 and PB-2 manned by 20 men of 9 Platoon, No. 3 Coy, HKVDC.

11. The battle for the two pillboxes started around 0620hrs on the 19th when a group of Japanese were spotted proceeding along Sir Cecil's Ride. 'For 10 min solid PB-1 opened fired at an estimated 400 enemy closely massed and unable to extend of take cover rapidly.' Maj. Stewart OC No. 3 Coy HKVDC's War Diary. By 0740hrs, the Japanese were 'in possession of the whole Jardine's Lookout area except PB-1 and 2s'. By 0830hrs the Japanese returned to take PB-1 and PB-2 using heavy mortar fire alternating with infantry attacks. Around noon, a Japanese party attempted to throw hand grenades through the loopholes of PB-1, but was wiped out by the defenders of PB-2, who came out to help. After all the guns of PB-1 had been knocked out, Lt. Field led his surviving men into the open and fought on with small arms. At about 1500hrs, Lt. Field ordered L/Cpl Broadbridge and 12 men to evacuate and held on with a few defenders. At 1800hrs, all the remaining defenders except L/Sgt. White had been wounded, some mortally. A Japanese officer came in with a flag of truce; the defenders finally surrendered. Those who could not walk were left to die.

BATTLE OF THE WONGNEICHONG GAP, 19 DECEMBER 1941

The loss of Wongneichong Gap was a battle that the British defenders never recovered from. The battle raged on for two days, although some pillboxes did not surrender until 22 December.

the 3/230th, eating lunch, incredibly without posting sentries. The Winnipeg Grenadiers wasted no time and inflicted heavy casualties. By 1745hrs the Winnipeg Grenadiers were only 100m short of Repulse Bay Road, to the south-south-east of the Gap. Hodkinson and four men with a 2in. mortar worked their way round the south-west spur of Mt Nicholson to reach the abandoned Brigade HQ, together with 20 walking wounded, and established a foothold at the Gap, while at the abandoned HQ, Hodkinson received orders from Fortress HQ to attack the police station at 2200hrs. Two HKVDC armoured cars with Vickers medium machine guns came in support but these were disabled by accurate enemy fire. Like Pinkerton, Hodkinson succeeded in getting close to his objective but was also seriously wounded. For this action Hodkinson was awarded the DSO.

By the morning of the 20th it was clear the Japanese had gained control of the Gap. However, elements of D Coy, Winnipeg Grenadiers, were still holding out in various pillboxes north of the Gap. Initially 17 and 18 Platoons were in a forward position with Coy HQ and 16 Platoon to the rear, located across Wongneichong Road almost directly opposite to brigade HQ. The forward positions were soon overwhelmed and cut off from the rest of the company. They fought on leaderless until they withdrew to the battalion's HQ. With Capt. A. S. Bowman, the OC, killed and second in command, Capt. R. W. Philips, wounded, the command of the company rested on Lt. T. A. Blackwood. An attempt to relieve D Coy by B Coy, Winnipeg Grenadiers, on the evening of the 20th failed, with heavy casualties, killing all the officers and 29 men. With less than 50 men, all wounded, Lt. Blackwood continued to inflict heavy casualties on the Japanese until 22 December when, exhausted and without ammunition or food and water, D Coy surrendered. D Coy killed more than 200 enemies. In a post-war report the Japanese refused to believe that only one company of Winnipeg Grenadiers had held the Gap. For their stubborn defence Philips and Blackwood were awarded the MC and three of their men were awarded the Military Medal.

The battle of the Wongneichong Gap was characterized by a lack of coordination and planning. On the night of the 19th/20th, no less than three separate companies attacked the police station with another company at Jardine's Lookout, all within the space of five hours, all separately organized and initiated by the local commander. Had it been possible to coordinate these individual actions into a single simultaneous attack, it seems possible that the objective set by Fortress HQ might have been met.

By the end of the 20th the British lost the vital ground of Wongneichong, except for Postbridge House, a large mansion in the area of Wongneichong Gap. For the Japanese, Wongneichong was the single most costly battle since the invasion; they suffered over 800 casualties and the CO of the 3/230th was seriously wounded.

BEGINNING OF THE END: 20–23 DECEMBER 1941

At dawn on 20 December the IJA was at the following positions:

- On the east side of Hong Kong, the 1/229th, the divisional reserve, and 2/228th were ready to advance from Taitam and Saiwan towards Stanley

- In the area around Stanley Gap – an area west of the Wongneichong Gap, south-east of the Jardine's Lookout, west of the reservoir the 2 and 3/229th were ready to turn south to Repulse Bay
- East of Wongneichong Gap, the 1/228th was ready to advance towards Deep Water Bay
- The 3/228th, one of the original reserve units, had just landed on the northern shore of Hong Kong
- On Jardine's Lookout, two battalions, 1 and 2/230th, were ready to advance west across the Gap.

At the same time, the West Brigade was holding an ill-defined defensive line with Z Coy, 1 Middlesex, and the remnants of the Rajputs at Leighton Hill in the north, 2 Royal Scots in the centre was holding the northern slope of Mt Nicholson and the Winnipeg Grenadiers, less D Coy, was still holding pillboxes at Wongneichong Gap.

First to move was the 228th from Wongneichong, to clear Postbridge House of the remaining resistance. At the same time, the 229th sent a recce party past Violet Hill at the south of the reservoir to the cliff that overlooks the Repulse Bay Hotel, which was and still is a five-star beachside resort. In December 1941, the hotel not only housed its regular customers, but also evacuees, a mixture of soldiers and sailors, and the scene was set for an epic three-day siege. Despite having gained much ground, the Japanese later admitted that the opposition had been much stronger than they had anticipated, with the result they were forced to spend the 20th consolidating their positions, bringing up fresh supplies. For now the IJA was content to hold on to its captured positions.

The garrison was, however, not in a position to rest; Brig. Wallis sent a Royal Rifles of Canada company and two HKVDC platoons to the Repulse Bay Hotel in hope of attacking the Gap from the south via Violet Hill. This force soon recaptured the hotel garages and outhouses but without artillery support did not manage to get much beyond the hotel. Worried about the situation there, Maltby sent a vastly understrength A Coy, 2/14 Punjab, (only 25 strong) to help and proceed along the road on the south side of Hong Kong Island, but it was held up at Shouson Hill (just north of Deep Water Bay, north-east of today's Ocean Park), trying to link up with the 20 or so sailors held up on the summit in two houses. Colonel Kidd the CO of 2/14 Punjab, with a mixed force of sailors and Punjabis, personally led the assault on Shouson Hill (150m). Kidd was killed and the mixed force failed and retreated with heavy losses. By the 22nd, after moving from Shouson Hill, the Japanese succeeded in taking

The IJA advancing along Electric Road on Hong Kong Island. The abandoned wooden carriages are most likely horse-drawn ammunition or supply baggage train, something rarely seen but which was a vital part of any army in the early 1940s. (Author's collection)

IJA PACK HOWITZER ARTILLERY MOVING UP A MOUNTAIN PATH IN HONG KONG (PP. 72–73)

An IJA 37mm RF (rapid-fire) gun carried by a packhorse is seen here, moving up Sir Cecil's Ride. Most likely this is part of the 2nd Independent RF Gun (anti-tank) Artillery Battalion. The term RF was used to confuse foreigners about the true nature of the weapon.

The 37mm gun was known as Type 94 37mm RF gun **(1)** and could be broken down into four parts, each carried by a packhorse. Each battery had two gun troops and one ammunition/maintenance troop. The gun troop was commanded by an officer, usually a lieutenant. Under him were two sections, each with a gun and an ammunition team.

Each gun was crewed by a team of eight with a junior NCO, usually a corporal, in command who issued orders and positions the gun. Under him was his gun crew of seven:

Crewman No. 1: moved the gun, sets the trail, sets up the breech block.

Crewman No. 2: was responsible for the cleaning rod and moving the gun into position. If there was a misfire crewman No. 2 would retrieve it using the extra firing cord.

Crewman No. 3: moved the gun, set the trail, set up the breech block, adjusted the height, open and shut the breech block, loaded the gun and retrieved the empty cases.

Crewman No. 4: sets the sight and prepares the gun position as well as firing the gun.

Crewman No. 5: carried the gun-sight and also carried a toolkit.

Crewman No. 6: carried the second toolkit and prepared the ammunition.

Crewman No. 7: carried one round for immediate use and helped to fuse the shell, as well as assisting Crewman No. 6.

Crossing ahead of the gun crew is a Type 92 7.7mm medium machine-gun crew **(2)**. The gun was effective to 4,300m with 450 rounds per minute and is being handled by a crew of ten with two horses, supported by an ammunition section of ten men and eight horses.

The gun crew leader, also known as the gun No. 1 (not seen in this plate), was usually a sergeant and usually carried the gun toolkit and a pick. The pick was to set the position of the gun, the job of the section leader.

The gun No. 2 was usually a lance-corporal, and was also the second in command. He was responsible for loading the gun and carried part of the Type 96 sight.

Gun crew No. 3 was usually a senior private soldier. He carried another part of the Type 96 sight and his job was to assist the section leader.

No. 4 was the actual gunner, usually a private first class. He carried the toolkit and also a part of the Type 94 sight.

Gun crewmen Nos. 5–8 were usually ammunition carriers, each ammunition box carrying 600 rounds (only two are seen in this plate).

Gun crewmen Nos. 9–10 were horse handlers and usually tasked with carrying extra ammunition and tools as well as the spare barrel. This item is not shown in the plate.

Brick Hill (where Ocean Park is today) held by elements of 1 Middlesex and a nearby HKSRA Bty.; they proceeded to behead all survivors.

Despite the success in pushing back the British on all fronts, much of the ground that the Japanese had conquered contained pockets of stubborn resistance. The HKSRA was still hanging on at one end of Brick Hill. A mixed bag of HKVDC, Navy, Canadians and Middlesex under Maj. Dewar were holding on to Little Hong Kong's ammunition store. In the meantime HMS *Cicala* was holding a position in Deep Water Bay providing artillery support; however, it was hit from the air and scuttled, eventually sinking in the Lamma Channel.

The West Brigade was also developing a counter-attack. Colonel H. B. Rose, CO of the HKVDC, took over West Brigade after the death of Lawson and used much of the 20th to prepare a plan for the next day. His plan was for 2 Royal Scots and the Winnipeg Grenadiers to attack towards the Gap from the west. B Coy, Winnipeg Grenadiers, under Maj. G. Trist was brought up from Pokfulam on the west coast of Hong Kong Island and was to join up with the Scots. The attack got off to a bad start. B Coy was late moving off as it waited in vain for 2 Royal Scots who for some unknown reason had already moved off from the eastern slopes of Mt Nicholson. The Winnipeg Grenadiers were thus left alone to mount the attack in pitch darkness and pouring rain. Split into two, they circled Mt Nicholson from opposite directions and met above the Gap where they were to assemble and attack on the morning of the 21st. Also for some unknown reason, the summit of Mt Nicholson was left unoccupied and Col. Doi once again demonstrated his aggressiveness; in a snap decision he ordered the 1/228th in a three-company forward formation to take advantage of this lapse in concentration and, using heavy rain as cover on the afternoon of the 20th, took the summit without opposition. B Coy stumbled on the three companies of Japanese and a fierce firefight developed that cost the Winnipeg Grenadiers all its officers; the CSM, seven NCOs and 29 men also became casualties. Facing an overwhelming force, B Coy was forced to withdraw to the west side of Mt Nicholson. Meanwhile Doi was preparing to follow up this success and assault Mt Cameron.

As dawn broke on the 21st, Wallis came up with a new plan to attack the Gap, this time in coordination with Rose. Wallis was to bring D Coy, Royal Rifles of Canada, and No. 1 Coy, HKVDC, and one medium machine-gun section from No. 2 Coy, HKVDC, together with the two remaining Bren carriers, all under the command of Maj. T. G. MacAuley Royal Rifles of Canada, to move on Wongneichong. Moving off from Stanley Mount at 0915hrs the group soon encountered accurate mortar fire from Red Hill; the Canadians were soon engaged in hand-to-hand fighting at the summit of Bridge Hill and the HKVDC on Notting Hill, two features that had to be secured before pushing to the Gap via Violet Hill. By 1700hrs, MacAuley, as well as all the officers of the HKVDC, had been wounded. Wallis had no choice but to withdraw. Opposing Wallis was an overwhelming IJA force, which amounted to two battalions, 1/229th and 1/230th, backed up by artillery and three tankettes.

Taking advantage of the chaos, the Japanese mounted another landing at 1030hrs on the 21st and pushed towards Victoria City, reaching the east side of what is today's Victoria Park. In the process an anti-aircraft gun manned by No. 6 Bty. HKVDC at the Watson's factory in Causeway Bay was knocked out. Heavy mortar fire rained on the naval yard and all guns were put out of action.

Major C. R. Templer, formerly of 30th Coastal Bty., was ordered by Maltby to take command of the situation at Repulse Bay. Having succeeded in holding off numerous probing attacks, Templer was ordered by Maltby to attack the Gap with two platoons of Royal Rifles of Canada, one from HQ Coy and one from C Coy, with two of the HKVDC's Vickers medium machine guns and two trucks. On the way, Templer gathered two more platoons from A Coy, Royal Rifles of Canada, that were on Middle Ridge, but then he saw the size of force that the Japanese had in the area of the Gap and decided to cancel the planned attack and withdraw to the far side of the ridge.

At daybreak on the 22nd, the IJA finally managed to bring heavy artillery to Hong Kong Island. The IJA had two battalions of the 229th in the Repulse Bay area attacking the hotel. Two of the three divisional reserves, 1/229th and 1/230th, were deployed against East Brigade, which by the 22nd was establishing the last line of defence around Stanley Peninsula. The defences of Stanley were divided into three areas: in the forward area was Lt. Col. Home with elements of 1 Middlesex, B, C, D Coy, Royal Rifles of Canada, and No. 2 Coy, HKVDC, supported by a single 2-pdr under 965 Bty. In the second line of defence located at Stanley village under Lt. Col. Wilcox were elements of B and D Coy, 1 Middlesex, under the command of Capt. M. P. Weedon, survivors from No. 1 Coy, HKVDC, and Stanley Platoon HKVDC supported by two 18-pdr and 2-pdr guns. Finally at the reserve area at Stanley Hill and Fort under Lt. Col. S. Shaw were 1 and 2 Bty. HKVDC with 30 and 36 Bty. RA fighting as infantry, supported by two 18-pdr, two 3.7in. howitzers under Maj. Forrester as well as 9.2in. and 6in. coastal guns.

Over on the west, British forces were barely holding on. C Coy, 2/14 Punjab, were holding the northern position, followed by Z Coy, 1 Middlesex, on Leighton Hill. South of Z Coy were B Coy 4/7 Rajputs, followed by B Coy, 2/14 Punjab to the south of the Rajputs. The Royal Scots and C Coy, Winnipeg Grenadiers, were in the area of Mt Cameron. South of Mt Cameron were D and B Coy, Winnipeg Grenadiers, and finally on the southern coast of Hong Kong Island was a mixed bag of British and HKVDC.

By noon the Japanese launched an attack on Stanley Mound (386m) and Sugarloaf, both occupied by B Coy, Royal Rifles of Canada, augmented with one platoon from HQ Coy, Royal Rifles of Canada, and two platoons from D Coy, Royal Rifles of Canada. Despite repulsing the Japanese several times the Canadians were forced to retire to the southern slopes of Stanley Mound when ammunition ran low. In the meantime the situation at Repulse Bay Hotel was deteriorating fast, but Maj. Templer was still able to hold out, despite many assaults there.

With resistance at Wongneichong finally over, the Japanese focused on taking Mt Cameron. The situation was desperate; Mt Cameron overlooked Wanchai Gap, the site of West Brigade's

Japanese troops of the right flank advancing along Mt Butler and the Jardine's Lookout area. In the background is the Kowloon Peninsula. The tall structure at the tip of the peninsula at Tsim Sha Tsui is the clock tower of the Kowloon–Canton Railway Terminus. This clock tower still stands today. (Hong Kong Library)

new HQ as well as the Winnipeg Grenadiers battalion HQ. The Japanese were concentrating in large numbers of troops on a front just over a kilometre long, in the area between the lower southern slopes of Mt Cameron and Little Hong Kong. Colonel Rose brought up Nos. 4 and 7 Coys, HKVDC, to a line running from Wanchai Gap to Mt Kellet. During the afternoon there was a very strong attack on the area held by the 2/14 Punjab's B Coy (under Maj. Kampta Prasad), who were beaten back and reduced to only eight men with two light machine guns. A gap was opened up between the Punjabis and Scots, but B Coy 4/7 Rajputs' counter-attack hit at the Japanese flank and prevented the gap from getting worse. The Middlesex moved up to fill the gap in the line. The IJA attacked positions south of Mt Cameron but was driven off by D Coy, Winnipeg Grenadiers.

Any further westward penetration by the Japanese would result in further isolation of the remaining troops. Elements of 1 Middlesex (only 40 strong), 2/14 Punjab and 5/7 Rajputs were still holding out at Leighton Hill and the racecourse. Major G. Trist, battalion second in command, was ordered to take command of a mixed force of about 100 members of C Coy, Winnipeg Grenadiers, later reinforced by 30 sappers to counter the Japanese westward move. The sapper platoons and two Winnipeg Grenadiers platoons were placed on the right under Lt. H. L. White. Three platoons of Winnipeg Grenadiers under Capt. N. O. Bardal (acting OC A Coy) were under intensive artillery bombardment and, without entrenching tools, were hit hard, and by 2200hrs the Japanese broke through on the right and worked through to the rear, trying to surround the Canadians, but the Canadians managed to withdraw to Mt Gough and escape encirclement.

On the 23rd the situation in the urban parts of the island had also become critical. The Rajputs who were on the right of 1 Middlesex at Leighton Hill had been heavily bombed and fell back at 0800hrs, exposing the Middlesex right flank. Rapidly the Japanese infiltrated around 1 Middlesex and together with heavy mortar managed to destroy all the remaining positions.

By this time the Japanese had advanced far enough to cut off the main water supply to Victoria. Pipes were damaged and key water reserves were in the hands of the Japanese; water shortage was beginning to hit both civilians and troops. Without water it was just a matter of time before the British had to capitulate.

LAST CHRISTMAS: 24–25 DECEMBER 1941

Christmas Eve arrived with all the defenders in unenviable situations. In Stanley the Royal Rifles of Canada, who had borne the brunt of the attacks, were withdrawn into Stanley Fort, but not before a heated meeting between Lt. Col. Home and Brig. Wallis, in which the Canadians accused the rest of the brigade of not 'pulling their weight' in the battle. With the Royal Rifles of Canada back in the fort, the Stanley defences were reorganized. No. 2 Coy, HKVDC, was at Chung Homkok. Stanley Platoon, HKVDC, under Lt. Fitzgerald was north-east of the Stanley police station. Middlesex with its medium machine guns was in the pillboxes surrounding No. 1 bungalow, with a small force of the Royal Rifles of Canada towards Taitam Road by Pillbox 27. Stanley village was held by ten men of No. 2 Coy, HKVDC. The second line of defence ran across Stanley Peninsula close to the

British troops waiting to be marched into s POW camp. The man on the right is probably a sailor. In December 1941, the weather in Hong Kong was quite cold and thus long sleeves and long trousers were definitely a must. (Author's collection)

Battle of Hong Kong anniversary parade in front of the cricket pavilion, since demolished. The soldier in the centre wears an old-style backpack, with wooden frame and Korean ox-hide cover for waterproofing, identified by its central vertical straps. On the right is the newer 1938-model backpack, made entirely of cloth fastened with two parallel straps. (Hong Kong Library)

north of St Stephen's College with the police station defended by British, Chinese and Indian policemen with Lewis guns and grenades. With the policemen was No. 1 Coy, HKVDC, and, with all the officers and senior NCOs gone, it was left to Cpl. E. C. Drown to take command. Finally, the last line of defence running across St Stephen's Prep School just north of the prison was held by one section of No. 1 Coy, HKVDC, under Sgt. Murphy and 1 Bty. HKVDC under Capt. F. G. Rees.

By this stage European prison staff, wardens and even prisoners were incorporated into the HKVDC. An unofficial commander was prisoner 'Crumb' Chattey, formerly captain and adjutant of 1 Middlesex, who had been court-martialled and was serving a two-year sentence for homosexual offences, according to the law of the times. Chattey took charge of 40 jailers and assorted men, including the colony hangman who put up a spirited fight.

The Japanese were massing troops on Taitam Road with the obvious intention of crushing the remaining defence at Stanley; the attack failed but not before destroying two 18-pdrs belonging to 965 Bty. and two 2-pdrs at Deep Water Bay. Just short of 2100hrs, the second attack began, this time supported by three tankettes. Two were destroyed by the 2-pdrs but, in the skirmish, No. 2 Coy, HKVDC, was forced back to Stanley village losing most of its men on the way. Major H. R. Forsyth the OC of No. 2 Coy was recommended for a VC by Wallis for his stubborn defence against overwhelming odds. Soon after midnight, the pillbox manned by C Coy, 1 Middlesex, was overrun; Sgt. Sheehan and his crew were killed, with the exception of Pte. Foley, 1 Bty. The HKVDC line broke and the IJA overran St Stephen's College, which was now an overcrowded temporary hospital and proceeded to commit the sadistic massacre and rape of all occupants. Eventually the Japanese broke through the eastern side of the prison and by dawn they reached Tweed Bay and St Stephen's Prep School and the defenders were reconciled to a last stand on Christmas Day.

On Christmas morning Brig. Wallis ordered C Coy, Royal Rifles of Canada, to lead a counter-attack to establish a line on the high ground north of the fort by retaking the bungalows on the ridge in Stanley village. Lieutenant-Colonel Home of the Royal Rifles of Canada refused to obey the order and Wallis instead deployed D Coy, Winnipeg Grenadiers, under Maj. Parker to lead the attack. At 1300hrs the attack went in, unsupported by artillery. The 18th Platoon under

Sgt. McDonnell penetrated as far as Stanley village, inflicting heavy loss on the Japanese in hand-to-hand fighting but was eventually forced back to the fort. Of the 148 who started the attack only 44 answered roll-call at the end.

In urban areas, through clever use of mines and the use of a Bofors L60 40mm in an anti-personnel capacity, the 230th Regt. advanced into the Wanchai and was held up at the China Fleet Club. At Wanchai Market, 965 Bty.'s 18-pdr was destroyed and soon the Japanese

Living conditions in Stanley Civil Internees Camp. Mr A. Raven from Yorkshire and Mrs Tribble from Somerset, whose husband was in the Hong Kong Civil Service, enjoying the first square meal after the arrival of Rear-Adm. Harcourt in Hong Kong. (IWM)

reached the western boundary of the Naval Dockyard. The Rajputs were pushed back west of the racecourse and Mt Parish fell, leaving the way to Victoria City open to the Japanese.

At 1530hrs on 25 December, Governor Young officially surrendered. A white flag was raised and Mark Young with Maj. Gen. Maltby crossed the harbour from Queen's Pier and officially surrendered to Sakai. They met at the Peninsula Hotel, now named the 'Toa' by the Japanese. Lieutenant-Colonel R. G. Lamb Royal Engineers and Lt. J. T. Prior drove down from Fortress HQ to Stanley to order Wallis to surrender. Wallis refused to obey without written instruction. Major Harland, the Brigade Major 2 Royal Scots, was sent to get written confirmation. At 0230hrs on 26 December 1941, Wallis finally surrendered; he and 2,000 men walked across the lines.

On the 28th, the Japanese mounted a 2,000-man victory parade led by Lt. Gen. Sano on a white horse; while the general was parading, his troops were on three days of officially sanctioned 'R&R' of rape and pillage.

CHRISTMAS DAY DASH – THE ESCAPE OF REAR-ADMIRAL CHAN CHAK

Rear-Admiral Chan Chak, the 'one-legged' Chinese admiral, came to Hong Kong in 1938 under the guise of General Manager of Wah Kee & Co, a stockbroker who was in fact the head of the Chinese Military Mission in Hong Kong with the specific objective of coordinating China's war effort with the British. Chan was working closely with the police special branch and intelligence services to coordinate the activities of the Nationalist agents, many of whom were Triad members, and to winkle out Japanese sympathizers and traitors. Chan was assisted by Col. Yee Shiu Kee of the Chinese Secret Service (in disguise as an insurance salesman), Lt. Cdr. Henry Hsu as his aide de camp, and Coxswain Yeung Chuen as his bodyguard.

On the morning of 25 December 1941, Chan was given permission to command the remnants of the 2nd MTB Flotilla and a mixed party of civilians, soldiers and sailors to escape before the official signing of the unconditional surrender of British forces in Hong Kong, which was expected sometime in the

Last stand at Stanley 24–25 December 1941

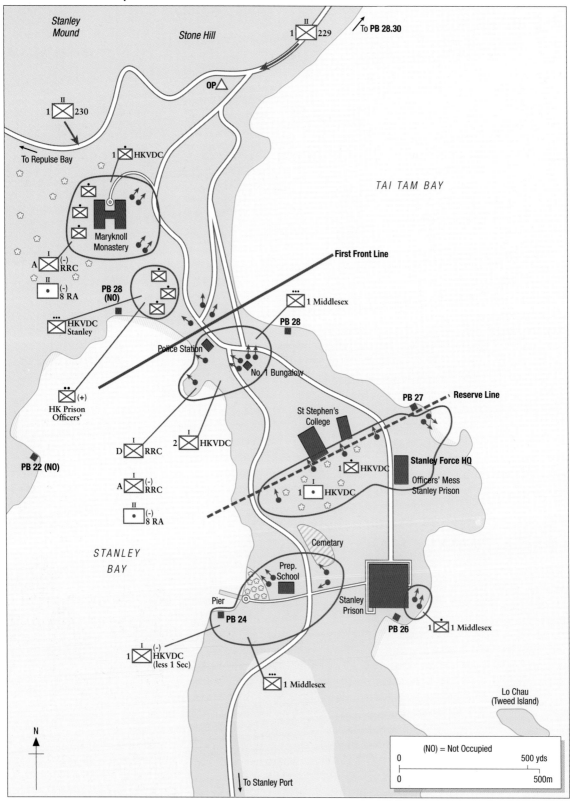

late afternoon. MTBs *7, 9, 10, 11* and *27* were at holding positions around the south side of Aberdeen Island waiting for Chan, who, after a precarious journey through the ruins of Victoria, eventually reached Aberdeen. On his arrival the MTBs were not to be seen and, instead, after searching around, he found HMS *Cornflower II*, the HKVDC's launch and decided to board it to search for the MTBs. In order to get out of the Japanese bombardment zone, the boat moved toward open sea, but IJA machine guns opened up and the launch was stopped. Abandon ship was called and Rear-Adm. Chan jumped in after removing his wooden leg and giving his lifebuoy to his non-swimming bodyguard Yeung. Just as Chan dived in with Hsu, the one-legged admiral was shot in the wrist – which made swimming with one arm and one leg almost impossible. Despite all odds Chan and Hsu attempted to land but were still under fire. By now the IJA was shooting tracers, trying to drive the two back down to the sea by setting alight the grass on the hill. Colonel Yee did not jump and was last seen on the bullet-riddled boat. Yee later managed to hide on Hong Kong Island for a few days before making his way to unoccupied China.

Every man for himself, the rest of the escapees scattered to various points on Aberdeen Island. On hearing the gunfire, the MTBs, which were hiding on the other side of Aberdeen Island, approached cautiously, rescuing survivors on the way, including Chan, Yeung and Hsu.

By 2130hrs on Christmas Day the 68 survivors were speeding towards Mirs Bay to meet up with the CCP guerrillas. On arriving, the MTBs were scuttled after all valuables had been retrieved. The CCP guerrillas were there to protect, guide and provide food and lodging to the escape party all the way to Huizhou in unoccupied China. Chen and his party were welcomed as heroes. This dramatic escape was the first of many and marked the beginning of cooperation between the Allies and the CCP guerrillas.

Rear-Admiral Chan meeting the Nationalist Chinese Generals of the 7th War Zone. From left to right, Deputy GOC Jiang Guangnai, David MacDougall (Ministry of Information), Cdr. Hugh Montague Royal Navy, Chinese Senior Officer, GOC Yu Hanmou, Rear-Adm. Chan Chak, Col. H. Owen-Hughes HKVDC and Chinese Chief of Staff Wang Zhun. (IWM)

Boy soldiers of the Hong Kong and Kowloon Independent Brigade (HKKIB), a sub-unit of the ERC that operated exclusively in Hong Kong. The HKKIB was formally established in a Catholic church in Sai Kung on 3 February 1942 with Cai Guoliang as commander and Chen Daming as commissar. (Author's collection)

EAST RIVER GUERRILLAS

As soon as the British withdrew from Kowloon, a new force, the Guangdong People's Anti-Japanese Guerrillas East River Column (ERC), took over the struggle against the Japanese invaders. Except for some heavy equipment that was destroyed, the British Army left behind a sizeable quantity of small arms and ammunition in Kowloon. Under the direction of Lin Ping, the party secretary of the Third and Fifth Column, 50 members infiltrated Hong Kong as early as 9 December 1941 to scavenge for

leftover weapons. The ERC was a pro-CCP force that was founded in 1938 by combining various local anti-Japanese forces in the South Guangdong area that sprang up after the capitulation of Guangzhou to the Japanese. Two key local guerrilla forces formed the core of the ERC – the Baoan People's Anti-Japanese Guerrilla Main Force, founded by Zeng Sheng, later the commander of the ERC, and East Baoan People's Anti-Japanese Guerrilla Regiment of Wang Zuorao (later Chief of Staff of the ERC).

Just before the invasion of Hong Kong, the Third and Fifth Column already had a force 1,500 strong. It was a battle-tested force that had been fighting the Japanese since 1938 in Guangdong Province. At the same time, Chinese Hong Kongers, mostly farmers and fishermen, also began to take up arms against the Japanese; by the end of December 1941 over 100 members of the ERC were active in Hong Kong and, in order better to organize the anti-Japanese guerrilla force, the HKKIB was formed in February 1942 and was commanded by Cai Guoliang with Chen Daming as the Political Commissar. Cai was to report to Zeng Sheng, the overall commander of the ERC.

ESCAPE AND EVASION

The first mission of the ERC was to rescue the many key Chinese and foreigners that were living in Hong Kong during 1941. While China was in flames, Hong Kong was still at peace. Many prominent Chinese, such as industrialists, politicians and authors as well as other VIPs came to the colony to escape the war. As early as 9 December 1941, on instruction from the highest authority of the Chinese Communists, the ERC was to rescue these selected VIPs and take them past Japanese lines to designated safe areas in China. From December 1941 to June 1942, over 800 key VIPs were rescued and escorted to safe areas. During this period the ERC also escorted over 2,000 overseas Chinese who came to China to fight in the anti-Japanese war.

The ERC also took an active part in rescuing POWs and aiding escapees. In March 1942, British POWs were forced to carry out hard labour in Kai-Tak Airport and the ERC successfully assigned English-speaking agents disguised as street vendors to infiltrate the airfield and rescue Capt. Thompson and four others through the rainwater culvert system. Other notable rescues included Lt. Col. Ride of the HKVDC, who went on to establish the British Army Aid Group (BAAG), numerous POWs and civilian internees. Amongst the military, notable escapees that were aided by the ERC included Lt. J. Douglas HKRNVR, Lt. J. W. Hursto Royal Navy, and Lt. G. D. Clagne RA, a number of Indian soldiers including Lashkar

In recognition of the help rendered by the ERC to the British, especially by the HKKIB, General Sir Neil Ritchie (seen seated in the middle) presented a commemorative banner to the Sai Kung Chamber of Commerce in a ceremony on 12 April 1947. (Author's collection)

Singh, Mehnga Singh HKSRA, civilian VIPs such as HSBC banker T. J. J. Fenwick, Police Superintendent W. P. Thompson, and key expatriates working in Hong Kong at the time, including a number of Russians, Danes and Norwegians. Most of these escapees were escorted to unoccupied China, but two Royal Scots soldiers, Joseph Gallaher and Daniel Hodges, remained with the ERC for six weeks, training the guerrillas, mainly in the use of British arms, medium machine guns, etc., making them some of the very few non-Chinese to be fighting with the Chinese Communist force.

RESCUING US PILOTS

From 1942 onwards the USAAF started to bomb Hong Kong periodically and these raids intensified from 1943. It was inevitable that planes would be shot down and the capture of any downed US pilot was a top priority for the Japanese. The ERC took the lead in rescuing downed pilots. On 11 February 1944, Flight Lt. Donald Kerr of 3rd Wing, 32nd Fighter Squadron, 14th Air Force was shot down while escorting 12 B-25s on a mission to bomb Kai Tak Airport. Kerr was amongst the 20 P-51 Mustang fighters that took off from Guilin (Kweilin). After shooting down one Japanese fighter, Kerr was hit and had to bail out and landed on the hills over a kilometre north of the airport. As all this happened in broad daylight, the Japanese mobilized several companies of soldiers to capture Kerr. Injured and desperate to escape, Kerr was at one point only 3m from the IJA, hidden from view by a large rock. An ERC boy soldier or messenger by the name of Li Shi, who was only 13 years old at the time, took it upon himself to lead Kerr to safety and eventually to a safe house after instructing his father, who was also a member of the ERC, to aid Kerr. Eventually Kerr was able to rest in a safe mountain cave on Ma On Mountain where he stayed for two weeks to recuperate. Food, warm clothing and medicine were brought to him by an English-speaking female guerrilla, Lin Zhan, before he was escorted all the way back to Guilin airbase. Before leaving, Kerr met with Zeng Sheng, who gave him a letter for Gen. Claire Chennault of the 14th Air Force. In view of the increasing number of US pilots that the ERC had to rescue, Zeng requested a liaison officer be posted with the column. A US Army officer by the name of Merrill Ady served as the first liaison officer, later replaced by Lt. B. G. Davis, who served until the end of the war.

Other notable rescues included the crew of a B-25 that crashed into Bias Bay (Daya Bay) on 24 May 1944, Lt. G. Laverell, Sgt R. D. Shank, Sgt. D. Conleg, Sgt. H. Ellis and in 1945 Lt J. Egan of the 14th Air Force, who led a 60-bomber raid, were rescued by the marine detachment of the HKKIB, as was 2nd Lt. M. J. Crehan US Navy.

Soon the ERC gained a reputation for being tough, dependable and disciplined fighters, compared with the Nationalist-controlled guerrillas,

On 11 June 1944, an underground pro-Chinese Communist newspaper, *Forward Press*, published a thank you letter from Flt. Lt. D. W. Kerr USAAF to the ERC, depicting his escape from the IJA in a series of hand-drawn cartoons. (Author's collection)

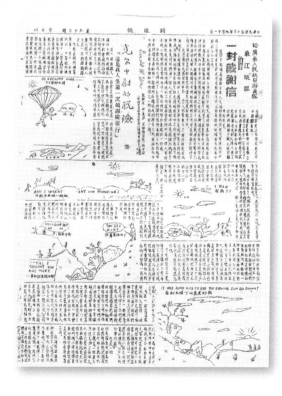

Flt. Lt. Donald Kerr seen here thanking Zeng Sheng, the leader of the ERC. Kerr is leaving the ERC and returning to Guilin airbase. Kerr's son, David, returned to China in 2008 to thank the ERC for saving his father. (Author's collection)

who were nothing more than local warlords, and the Allies began to cooperate with the ERC on an official basis. In 1944, as the USA was still debating the final strategy for the invasion of Japan, one of the options was to use China as a launch pad. As part of the preparation of this plan, the US military contacted the ERC to conduct intelligence gathering of Japanese depositions, local weather conditions as well as conducting target recces for air strikes and post-strike reports.

Throughout the war, the ERC not only had to contend with fighting the Japanese but also with sporadic skirmishes with the Nationalist guerrillas as well as the KMT Nationalist Army. In 1943, from the months of January to November, ERC conducted over 70 offensive actions and expanded to a force 3,000-strong, split into seven columns (No. 2, No. 3, No. 5, Huiyang Column, Baoan Column, HKKIB and the Escort Brigade). Amongst them the HKKIB attacked the Kai Tak Airport, destroyed the Argyle Road railway bridge, raided a Japanese armoury, captured and kidnapped Japanese and their allies, and killed and executed traitors. The ERC together with the Escort Brigade and the Independent Bias Bay column sunk a number of Japanese patrol craft and captured several vessels. By the end of the war in 1945, the ERC had expanded to an 11,000-strong force that was divided into nine columns and six independent battalions in four combat groups, namely East River, South River, Northern Guangdong and Eastern Advance Corps.

The formal surrender of the Japanese force in China took place on 9 September 1945, but the end of one war marked the beginning of another, the Chinese Civil War. The ERC officially withdrew from Hong Kong on 28 September 1945 and, as instructed by the CCP, immediately took the surrender of all Japanese forces in Guangdong; those Japanese forces and Japanese sympathizers that refused to surrender were destroyed. According to the American-sponsored 10 January 1946 ceasefire agreement, the warring Chinese factions agreed to halt any military action against each other and consolidated forces; according to the agreement all Communist forces were to move to north-east China and the Nationalist force would concentrate to the south. Under the supervision of the tri-party peacekeeping force (Chinese Nationalist, Chinese Communist and the US Army), 2,533 members of the ERC were allowed to be transported, by courtesy of the US Navy, to Yantai in Shandong Province, where they were absorbed into the CCP's Eastern China Field Army. However, despite the ceasefire agreement, the ERC was attacked in assembly areas, resulting in several deaths. The ERC story does not end here; the reputation of the ERC was such that the HKKIB, many of whom were local Hong Kong Chinese, were allowed to bear arms to assist the British authorities to maintain peace in the rural areas of Hong Kong until as late as September 1946.

From the formation of forces in 1938 until 1945, the ERC conducted offensive combat operations over 1,400 times, killed over 6,100 and captured over 3,500 Japanese soldiers or puppet government troops. It also suffered over 2,500 killed in action.

BRITISH ARMY AID GROUP (BAAG)

The British Army Aid Group was an MI9 organization set up by Lt. Col. Ride, the former OC of the Hong Kong Field Ambulance, with the aim of intelligence gathering and assisting POWs in escaping from the Japanese camps in Hong Kong. The BAAG is unique as the only British military organization that existed in the China theatre from 1942 onwards.

Shortly after being captured, while camp security was still lax, Ride and Lt. Morley, Sub-Lt. Davis, both HKRNVR, and L/Cpl. Francis Lee of the HKVDC escaped from Shamshuipo POW camp to Free China. The dramatic escape was carried out with the help of the ERC and it prompted Ride to help others do the same; he decided to form a group that became known as the BAAG. For his part in leading the escape, Ride was awarded an OBE and Francis Lee the Military Medal.

The BAAG also gathered military intelligence in southern China and Hong Kong. The agents of the BAAG, many of whom were ex-POWs, helped to facilitate the escape of more POWs. Towards the end of the war, the BAAG's influence reached as far as Hainan Island in south-west China, and it was engineering a mass escape of Australian POWs, under Operation *Man Friday*, which was cancelled on account of the Hiroshima bomb. The BAAG also conducted plenty of sabotage operations in Hong Kong. Before the onset of regular bombing by the US 14th Air Force, the BAAG conducted an unusual scheme to deny the Japanese ships repair facilities by bleeding dry the skilled labourers that were employed in the naval yard, through a strategy known as the 'Matey Scheme'. It helped these skilled labourers and artisans to escape and even found them jobs in India. In a very short time in the latter part of 1942, over 153 dockyard workers as well as their families had escaped.

In three years of operation the BAAG rendered assistance to 33 British and Allied escapees, 400 Indians (of whom 140 were in the armed forces), 40 downed US airmen, and 120 European and 550 Chinese civilians, enabling them to escape from Japanese-occupied Hong Kong. There were 128 escapees who were re-trained for further operations with the Chindits. The BAAG also played a part in famine relief and other humanitarian services, took an active role in the battle of Guilin and carried out demolition work as well as gathering vital intelligence for air and naval operations in the China theatre. Above all, through the BAAG an active British resistance was maintained in Hong Kong in defiance of the Japanese occupation.

This BAAG recce report depicts a Japanese machine-gun position on Leighton Hill, an area of high ground between Causeway Bay and Wanchai of Hong Kong Island. The building at the bottom right-hand side is Po Leung Kuk, a Chinese charity established for the protection of women and children. This building still stands today. (Author's collection)

A post-war photograph of Lt. Col. Lindsey Tasman Ride, founder of the BAAG, at a veterans' dinner. Note the BAAG unit emblem in the background. From 1948 to 1962 Ride served as colonel commandant of the Royal Hong Kong Defence Force. (Hong Kong Library)

A Royal Marine trooper is seen guarding Japanese prisoners. The Japanese soldier with his arms folded with a Star badge on his short sleeve is Lt. Col. Kanazawa, who was the head of the Kempetai, the feared Japanese 'Gestapo'. (Author's collection)

Surrender ceremony on 16 September 1945. To the right sits Maj. Gen. Okada Umekichi. Standing next to him in whites is Capt. Eccles, Royal Navy Head of Military Administration. Bending over Okada is Mr Makimura, a civil servant. Sitting opposite with hands clasped is Nationalist Chinese Maj. Gen. Pan Hwa Kuei, to his right is Adm. Sir Bruce Fraser, C-in-C British Pacific Fleet. (Author's collection)

THE SINKING OF THE *LISBON MARU*

After the capitulation, the Japanese soon began systematically to transport POWs to Japan for hard labour. The first batch of prisoners, some 700, had already been processed in the first week of September 1942. On 25 September another 1,834 prisoners were embarking the *Lisbon Maru* to Japan under the command of Lt. Walda of the IJA, while the vessel was under Capt. Koyda Shigeru. The prisoners were held in three holds, the Royal Navy in the forward hold, the Royal Scots, 1 Middlesex and other small units and individuals were in the second hold, which was just forward of the bridge, and the third hold, which was aft of the bridge, held members of the RA. Also on board were 778 Japanese soldiers, who occupied most of the deck space forward. As for all Japanese POWs, the accommodation was limited to say the least.

On the morning of 1 October 1942, at about 0400hrs, USS *Grouper* SS-214, a Gato-class submarine, was patrolling off the coast of western China close to Shanghai and spotted a target moving north. At 0704hrs USS *Grouper* let loose three Mk. 14 torpedoes at a range of approximately 3,000m; two missed and one hit amidships but did not explode because of faulty detonators – a problem which plagued the US Navy during this period of the war. A fourth torpedo was fired and it struck the stern of the ship, causing it to lose control and shudder to a halt.

The few prisoners who at that time were on deck were immediately pushed back into the nearest hold and Japanese sentries were placed at the entrance to each hold and began to batten down the hatches. Coastal patrol vessels immediately responded with depth charges, and the ship's 3in. deck gun began to fire spasmodically. At 0845hrs and 0937hrs, USS *Grouper* fired more torpedoes but missed both times; it was the last and seventh torpedo shot from stern tubes that found its mark and hit the *Lisbon Maru*.

During the whole period of the attack, many prisoners were suffering from dysentery and diarrhoea; without toilet facilities and fresh air, under tropical conditions, the situation could only be described as dire. Stewart, the CO of 1 Middlesex, remonstrated with the Japanese, requesting that they should at least leave one plank of timber to help provide a little air, but without success.

Number three hold was now taking in water and hand pumps were given to the prisoners. Some men, already weakened by disease, began to falter and a few died. Lieutenant Potter, a fluent Japanese speaker, broke free and approached Lt. Walda

requesting air and water but was refused. Later a Japanese ship came alongside, the Japanese soldiers were taken off and the *Lisbon Maru* was taken into tow. Almost 24 hours passed; the ship began to lurch and stagger. Since all requests had been ignored or refused, Lt. Col. Stewart authorized a small party to attempt to conduct a mass breakout. Men with homemade knives began to push them up through the planks of timber and began to cut away ropes and tarpaulins. Lieutenant Howell, Lt. Potter and others climbed onto the deck and proceeded towards the bridge, asking to be allowed to talk to Capt. Koyda, but the Japanese opened fire, killing Potter. The ship was by now very low in the water and evidently about to sink. It was every man for himself. Some of the POWs began to hack at the ropes and made a mad scramble for the narrow opening, with some falling and injuring themselves. Stewart immediately took hold of the situation, exclaiming: 'Steady the Middlesex. Remember who you are!' Immediately the NCOs took charge and order was soon established. At about 1030hrs, the *Lisbon Maru* finally sank. The Japanese soldiers and sailors, who were standing by aboard ships alongside, now began to fire at the POWs in the water. On the four or so Japanese ships standing by, no one made any attempt to assist the POWs. Some managed to climb alongside the Japanese vessels but, as they were clinging to the side or clambering on the gunwales, they were shot at or bayoneted.

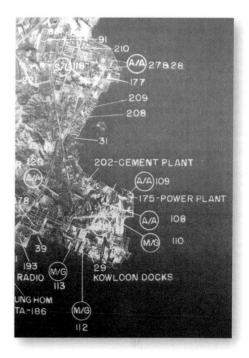

The US Army Air Force conducted extensive bombing of Hong Kong from 1942 onwards. This aerial photograph shows targeting information on the Kowloon Docks area. After the war this area was extensively reclaimed and forms roughly what is today's Hung Hom, Whampoa Gardens. (Author's collection)

After several hours, some of the stronger swimmers managed to get to the islands but many were lost in the water or sent crashing onto the rocks. At first Chinese fishermen on the islands did little to save the men from the sea, believing that they were Japanese, but on discovering they were Allied POWs they immediately sent boats out to the rescue. Eventually some 200 were picked up and taken to the Zhoushan Islands. POWs were treated with great kindness and given what little food the fishermen had and all of their clothing.

On 5 October, roll-call was taken in Shanghai; of the original 1,834 prisoners, 828 had perished. It was learned later that three men had managed to escape. On 7 October, 35 of the worst dysentery patients were left in Shanghai and the remainder were taken aboard the SS *Shinsei Maru* and SS *Washington Maru*; six died before reaching Japan. Finally, on the 10th, the POWs arrived at Moji and were immediately taken to Osaka where 50 more very sick prisoners were dropped off at Kokura with a similar number at Hiroshima. Eventually 500 went on to Kobe and the remainder to Osaka. The winter of 1942 was especially bleak and 200 were to die mostly from neglect, diphtheria, diarrhoea, pneumonia and malnutrition.

LIBERATION

At 1500hrs on 29 August 1945, operating under code name Operation *Ethelred*, a British fleet with some 55 vessels including six aircraft carriers (HMS *Illustrious*, *Venerable*, *Vengeance*, *Chaser*, *Striker* and *Vindex*), two battleships (HMS *Anson* and *Duke of York*), three cruisers, six destroyers, five frigates, eight submarines, no less than 33 minesweepers and a host of other

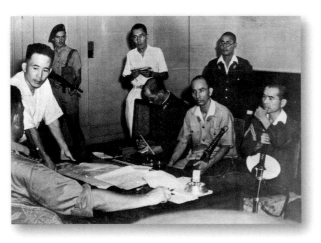

With his back towards the camera, Capt. Eccles Royal Navy, a fluent Japanese speaker, is dictating terms to the IJA at the Peninsula Hotel while Capt. Shimauchi (on the right-hand side), Lt. Col. Kanazawa (centre) and Maj. Shies, head of the local police, take notes. Eccles said, 'We have come here as conquerors, you will do as we say.' (Author's collection)

Japanese suicide boats and crew, surrendering to the men HMS *Whirlwind* and *Quadrant* in Picnic Bay, Lamma Island. Picnic Bay is better known today as Sok Ku Wan. Caves hiding the suicide boats can still be seen in the area. (IWM)

auxiliary ships led by Rear-Admiral Harcourt arrived just outside Hong Kong after two days steaming from Subic Bay in the Philippines. Harcourt was waiting for the final act of diplomatic negotiation before entering Hong Kong to take the surrender of the Japanese force. Whilst the fleet was waiting, the minesweepers were busy clearing a safe channel into Victoria Harbour and the accompanying Marines were busy clearing the outlying islands of Japanese forces, including de-arming a fleet of suicide boats that had been prepared to target the British liberation fleet. As the fleet entered the narrow channels approaching Victoria Harbour, three suicide boats came towards them. Taking no chances, covering fighters of the Fleet Air Arm blasted them out of the water.

As part of the preparation for the arrival of the British force, an Avenger with an escort of four Hellcats from HMS *Indomitable* headed for Kai Tak Airport to pick up a Japanese liaison officer, Makamura from the Ministry of Foreign Affairs, and his escort, ex-POW Cdr. Craven Royal Navy, to prepare for the formal entry of Harcourt's fleet into Hong Kong. On 30 August 1945, around midday, a fleet of minesweepers headed for the Lyemun Channel, followed by the destroyer HMS *Kempenfeldt*, cruiser HMS *Swiftsure* (to which Harcourt transferred the flag), followed by HMS *Euryalus*, HMCS *Prince Robert* (the same ship that brought C Force to Hong Kong in 1941) and finally Submarine Depot ship HMS *Maidstone*. Sub-Lieutenant William K.L. Lore, a Canadian–Chinese serving in the Royal Canadian Navy, became the first British officer to land on Hong Kong and proceeded to liberate Shamshuipo POW camp with a group of Marines.

However, the liberation of Hong Kong involved a lot more than just freeing the POWs and civilian detainees. Political manoeuvring at the last minute delayed the signing of the deeds of surrender. Behind the scenes there was the issue of who should be the Allied representative for the surrender ceremony. According to the 1943 Cairo Conference and orders from General MacArthur, Commander-in-Chief US Army Forces Pacific (AFPAC), Japanese forces in Hong Kong were to surrender to Chinese National Forces under Chiang Kai-shek, then the leader of wartime China. Chiang was hoping President Truman would back China's demand to receive the Japanese surrender in Hong Kong as the sole representative of Allied powers and thus enable China to reclaim Hong Kong from Britain. This diplomatic move was unsuccessful, Chiang was able to obtain only the concession of having a Chinese general attend the ceremony and this was a rare occasion when the Chinese flag flew alongside the British Union flag. This diplomatic manoeuvring delayed the formal ceremony of surrender at Government House until 16 September 1945.

AFTERMATH

There is no definitive casualty list for the battle of Hong Kong. Today it is accepted that Maltby's post-war dispatches of 2,123 dead or missing and 1,332 wounded for the defenders were grossly overestimated, while the Chief Signal Officer, whilst a POW, compiled a list with 2,721 recorded as dead and missing were considered as more an accurate estimate. Post-war estimates give 1,600 including casualties from those members of St John Ambulance that were attached to the garrison medical units. Civilian casualties were estimated to be as high as 7,000. Japanese Defence Agency historical section records show that 1,720 died in Hong Kong, while *Hong Kong News*, an English-language newspaper published by the Japanese occupation authority, on 29 December 1941 listed 1,966 dead and 6,000 wounded.

After Hong Kong, the 38th Division IJA was deployed to the Philippines (228th), Vietnam (229th and one battalion of 230th) and then to the Dutch East Indies in early 1942, and later to Guadalcanal in October 1942 where it took heavy losses. Lieutenant Wakabayashi, who led the attack on the Shing Mun Redoubt, was killed on 14 January 1943.

By 20 February 1942 the Japanese had appointed a new Governor, Maj. Gen. Isogai Rensuke, along with new garrison troops commanded by Brig. Okada Umekichi. The occupation troops were the independent 67th, 68th and 69th Infantry Regiments under Maj. Hirota Yoshitaka, Capt. Nakagawa Kanemitsubishi and Lt. Col. Yamashita Kazuo respectively. The artillery element was commanded by Col. Kawagawa Hisakatsu.

Japanese soldiers were often accused of committing war crimes during their operations and the 38th Division was no different. The commander of the infantry element of the division, Maj. Gen. Ito, was convicted of war crimes by the Allies after the war. Lieutenant-General Sakai, commander of the 38th Army who led the invasion of Hong Kong and subsequently served as temporary governor, was tried as a war criminal and executed by a firing squad in

Raising the Union flag at Governor's House, Hong Kong. Royal Navy sailors and Royal Marine troopers are seen assembled at the bottom of the picture, while Indian troops and possibly released ex-POW senior officials flank both sides of the Gate House. (Hong Kong)

1946. Major-General Isogai, Governor of occupied Hong Kong, was imprisoned for life for war crimes, but was released in 1967. Lieutenant-General Tanaka, the final Japanese Governor who was also concurrently the commander of the 23rd Army, was executed in 1947 for war crimes conducted in China. Of the senior Japanese commanders involved with the Hong Kong Campaign only Vice-Adm. Niimi survived the war, and he lived until he was 106.

Japanese Ministry of Foreign Affairs' envoy Makimura was the first Japanese to make contact with Rear-Adm. Harcourt. Here Makimura is seen being escorted by armed guards from HMS *Indomitable* after meeting with Rear Adm. Harcourt. (IWM)

HMHS *Oxfordshire*, built by Harland & Wolff, Northern Ireland was a commercial-turned-hospital ship that saw service in both world wars. It was finally scrapped in 1958. In this picture it is seen moored on the western docks in Kowloon, close to today's Ocean Centre and Ocean Terminal in Tsim Sha Tsui. (IWM)

IJN *Isuzu*, the flagship of Niimi, later fought in the Solomon Islands campaign and battles for Leyte Gulf, but was eventually sunk by US submarines on 7 April 1945 off Sumbawa, in the Java Sea. The second flagship IJN *Uji* continued in service in and around Chinese waters until the defeat of Japan. It was awarded as a war prize to the Nationalist Chinese Navy and renamed *Chang Chi*. During the Chinese civil war the crew defected to the CCP and renamed it *Nan Chang*.

Major-General Maltby spent the rest of the war first in Hong Kong and later in Shanghai and Taiwan before transferring to a camp near the Chinese–Mongolian border, and finally to Shenyang (Mukden) China. Late in 1946 Young resumed his post as Governor and believed that a lack of support for the British war effort from the Chinese had contributed to the rapid loss of Hong Kong. Post-war he tried installing a degree of representative government in Hong Kong. London was alarmed and soon replaced him with a new governor, Sir Robert Black. Young retired in 1947. Soon after, having returned to Britain, Maltby also retired from the Army. No recognition was bestowed on him, despite the stubborn defence he had put up in Hong Kong. The CO of 2 Royal Scots, Lt. Col. White, survived the war and returned to Britain but died soon after of cancer.

Rear-Admiral Chan was granted an honorary KBE, presented by Sir Horace Seymour, the British Ambassador to China. Colonel Yee was granted the dignity of an honorary CBE and Lt. Cdr. Henry Hsu was granted an honorary OBE. Lieutenant-Commander Hsu was a great athlete and, after the war, became an International Olympic Committee member representing Chinese Taipei.

Lieutenant-Colonel Stewart of 1 Middlesex died from illness in 1942. Petty Officer J. W. Fallace, W. C. Johnstone of the HKRNVR and Arthur Evans, a civilian employed by

the army, escaped from the *Lisbon Maru* and made it to Chongqing (Chunking) in Free China. Of the 1,834 POWs who boarded the *Lisbon Maru*, only 716 managed to return home. After the war, Lt. Walda was taken to the war crimes tribunal for brutal treatment of the POWs, but he died before he was sentenced. Captain Koyda, the captain of the *Lisbon Maru*, was sentenced to seven years' imprisonment.

The ERC was recognized by the British authorities; without its help none of the escapees would have survived the arduous journey to freedom. Questions were raised by the future British Prime Minister, the Rt. Hon. James Callaghan MP. As a result, generous monetary awards and free medical care were given to many surviving members and their families. Some were even given jobs in the public and private sectors and some chose to settle in the UK. The ERC liaison office eventually became the Hong Kong branch of the New China News Agency, in which many members of the ERC served until the return of Hong Kong to China in 1997. Zeng Sheng, the commander of ERC, later became the first Deputy Chief of staff of the South China Military Region, and then Deputy Provincial Governor and Mayor of Guangzhou. He was purged in the Cultural Revolution but was rehabilitated and rose to become Minister of Communication in 1979. Zeng died in Guangzhou in November 1995.

One hundred and twenty-eight Chinese members of the HKVDC, 49 Chinese members of the British Army, 50 Auxiliary Transport, ARP and other personnel managed to escape all the way to Free China and were transported by the RAF to Assam and then to Calcutta through the help of BAAG. The first two groups joined the 9th Battalion, the Border Regiment in Fort William, and the third and fourth groups joined the 1st Battalion, the Gloucestershire Regiment. These Hong Kong Chinese soldiers were at first not given any role but Brig. Michael Calvert stepped in, having served in Hong Kong and commanded the Chinese Sappers before 1941, and called for volunteers to fight the Japanese in Burma. All without exception stepped forward and after many months of hard training they were officially put into the war establishment on 14 February 1943 as part of Wingate's Chindits, the Hong Kong Volunteer Company.

After crossing from Kowloon, Sir Mark Young, the Governor, is greeted by Maj. Gen. Francis Festing GOC Land Forces Hong Kong, at Queen's Pier Hong Kong Island. Major-General Festing was twice GOC Hong Kong and later ended his career as Chief of Imperial General Staff and a field marshal. (IWM)

THE BATTLEFIELD TODAY

Modern Hong Kong is very different from the Hong Kong of 1941. However, parts of the 1941 battlefield remain almost unchanged. The Gin Drinkers Line, around the areas of the Shing Mun Redoubt and Golden Hill, overlooking Shing Mun reservoir, is located in what is now a country park. It is easily accessible by taxi and the city metro. (http://gwulo.com/shing-mun-redoubt)

The Hong Kong Museum of Coastal Defence, located in a Victorian fort overlooking the Leiyuemun (Lyemun) Channel, near Shaukeiwan on Hong Kong Island, which saw fierce battle during the night of 18 December 1941, can easily be reached by the city metro. (http://hk.coastaldefence.museum/index.php)

The areas among the Wongneichong Gap can be easily visited by bus from Central or by taxi. The bunkers in which Brig. Lawson fought his last battle are right next to the petrol station, across from the Hong Kong Cricket Club on Wongneichong Road. There is a battlefield trail that starts just opposite the entrance to Parkview Mansion. It loops along and down a hillside to pass an old anti-aircraft battery and a couple of pillboxes, then drops to the Gap itself, ending at the former bunker complex of Brig. Lawson.

There are a number of machine-gun bunkers dotted around the shores of Hong Kong Island that can still be seen. Most convenient are those that lined the shores of Repulse Bay Beach, on the south shores of Hong Kong Island. Although the guns are gone, the site of the batteries can still be seen, though only by car; Pinewood Battery, Victoria Peak on Hong Kong Island in what is now the Lung Fu Shan country park is a notable example. Badly damaged on 15 December 1941, it is one of the very few battle sites now standing virtually unchanged since 1941. Another site is the Devil's Peak Battery on Kowloon. You can take the Hong Kong metro to Yautong Station, followed by a short taxi ride.

Stanley Military Cemetery can easily be reached by car and is located near St Stephen's Bay in Stanley. Stanley village was one of the battlefields where the Royal Rifles of Canada, HKVDC, and 1 Middlesex, took the last stand. Fighting occurred in the cemetery itself on the afternoon of Christmas Day, when D Coy Royal Rifles of Canada tried to force the advancing Japanese from Bungalow C. Another worthwhile visit is the military cemetery located in Chaiwan, on the north-eastern corner of Hong Kong Island. The site of the cemetery is midway up Cape Collinson Road. A total of 1,528 soldiers, mainly from the Commonwealth, are buried here, including Brig. Lawson and Col. Hennessey.

The official British war memorial is a British-style cenotaph, exactly the same as that in London. It is located in Central, just next to the venerable Hong Kong Club. Behind the cenotaph, towards the sea, is the City Hall where, on adjoining ground, is a memorial garden with an octagonal hall that holds the book that bears all the names of those who fell during 1941–45. From 1962 to 1997, when the memorial garden was built, the book of the fallen contained only British war dead. The names of the Chinese ERC, who contributed so much to the war effort, were added only in 1997 after the change of sovereignty from Britain to China. Both of these monuments can easily be reached by the city metro.

There are two ERC monuments located in the New Territories, one in Wu Kau Tang and a second in Pak Tam Chung. Both are obelisks; the former is unique as it was the only monument bearing a CCP red star in colonial Hong Kong, and the latter is the biggest war monument in Hong Kong. Both can be reached only by car. In mainland China, a museum dedicated to the ERC is located in Guangdong Province, Dongguan City, Dalingshan Township. (http://www.dongzong.gov.cn/page/index.asp) A second, more easily reached museum, also dedicated to ERC, is located in Shenzhen, China, in Longgang District, Dongzhong Road, Huipo Zone. A small office, right in the heart of Shenzhen, was the former forward command post of the ERC. This office is located less than a five-minute walk from Laojie Metro Station in Shenzhen.

Stanley Internment Camp (now Stanley Prison) is out of bounds to visitors. St Stephen's College, a private college, can be visited only with special permission. The sites of North Point Camp, Shumshuipo POW camp, Ma Tau Chung and Argyle Street Camp have all been rebuilt with no trace of their former use.

Top left, the cenotaph, Hong Kong, Remembrance Day 2011; top right, the regimental cap badge of the HKVDC. Bottom centre, Memorial Garden, City Hall; the hexagonal building in the centre houses the names of all who died in the battle of Hong Kong 1941–45. (Author's collection)

FURTHER READING

Birch, Alan, and Cole, Martin, *Captive Christmas – The Battle of Hong Kong, December 1941* (1982)

——, *Captive Years – The Occupation of Hong Kong 1941–45* (1982)

Branham, Tony, *Not the Slightest Chance – The Defence of Hong Kong 1941* (2003)

——, *The Sinking of the Lisbon Maru* (2006)

Bruce, Phillip, *Second to None – The Story of the Hong Kong Volunteers* (1991)

Carew, Tim, *Fall of Hong Kong* (1960)

Chan, King Tong, Yau, Rosa, and Chan, Sunny K. L. (eds), *The Defence of Hong Kong* (2004) – a collection of essays on the Hong Kong–Kowloon Brigade of the East River Column

Chen, Dun De, *History of the Eight Route Army Office in Hong Kong* (2012) – *Chinese-language publication*

Chen, Sui-Jeung, *East River Column – Hong Kong Guerrillas in the Second World War and After* (2009)

Endacott, G. B., *Hong Kong Eclipse* (1978)

Felton, Mark, *The Coolie Generals – Britain's Far Eastern Military Leaders in Japanese Captivity* (2008)

Ferguson, Ted, *Desperate Siege – The Battle of Hong Kong* (1980)

Greenhous, Brereton, *'C' Force to Hong Kong – A Canadian Catastrophe 1941–1945* (1997)

Keung, Ko Tim, and Wordie, Jason, *Ruins of War – A Guide to Hong Kong's Battlefields and Wartime Sites* (1996)

Kwong, Chi-Man, and Cai, Y. L., *Lonely Outpost – The Battle of Hong Kong in the Pacific War* (2013) – Chinese language publication

Lindsay, Oliver, *At the Going Down of the Sun – Hong Kong and SE Asia 1941–1945* (1981)

——, *The Battle for Hong Kong 1941–1945 – Hostage to Fortune* (2006)

Luard, Tim, *Escape from Hong Kong – Admiral Chan Chak's Christmas Day Dash 1941* (2012)

Nakanishi, Ritta, *Japanese Infantry Arms in WWII* (1998)

——, *Japanese Military Uniforms 1930–1945* (1991)

Rekishi Gunzou, *Japanese Army Southern Operations*, Archive Volume 23 (2012)

Renfrew, Barry, *Forgotten Regiments – Regular and Volunteer Units of the British Far East* (2009)

Ride, Edwin, *BAAG – Hong Kong Resistance 1942–1945* (1981)

Roland, Charles G., *Long Night's Journey into Day – Prisoners of War in Hong Kong and Japan 1941–1945* (2001)

Snow, Philip, *The Fall of Hong Kong: Britain, China and the Japanese Occupation* (2004)

Vincent, Carl, *No Reason Why – The Canadian Hong Kong Tragedy: An Examination* (1981)

Wight-Nooth, George with Adkin, Mark, *Prisoner of the Turnip Head* (1994)

Xu, Lan, *Great Britain and the Sino-Japanese War 1931–1941* (2010) – *Chinese-language publication*

INDEX

Figures in *italic* refer to illustrations